The Festival Cookbook

Four Seasons of Favorites

The Festival Cookbook

Cookbook

Four Seasons of Favorites

Phyllis Pellman Good

Good Books

Intercourse, Pennsylvania 17534

Acknowledgments

Design and seasonal symbols by Craig N. Heisey.
Cover photo by Jonathan Charles.
Many friends contributed favorite recipes and memories about them to this collection celebrating the good earth and times of human gathering. Several recipes are from the late Doris Longacre, who contributed significantly to the matter of conscientious cooking and eating.

The Festival Cookbook: Four Seasons of Favorites
©1983, 1987 by Good Books, Intercourse, PA 17534
International Standard Book Number: 0-934672-57-1
Library of Congress Catalog Card Number: 87-25213
Originally published, 1983
Revised edition, 1987

Library of Congress Cataloging-in-Publication Data

The Festival cookbook.
    Includes index.
    1. Cookery, American. I. Good, Phyllis Pellman, 1948-
TX715.F426   1987   641.5   87-25213
ISBN 0-934672-57-1

Table of Contents

Introduction

The Festival Cookbook: Four Seasons of Favorites is a collection of favorite recipes gathered from Mennonite peoples scattered across North America. Once a primarily Germanic group, Mennonites are today diverse in their cultural backgrounds and increasingly influenced by the flavor of their surroundings.

This mix of recipes includes Pennsylvania Dutch Chicken Corn Soup and Vietnamese Chicken Salad, Russian Mennonite Porzelky and Habichuelas (Beans in Sauce). Here, then, is reflected our traditional past and our multi-cultural present.

These are some of our favorite foods today—thus the "Festival" in this cookbook's title. I asked friends for recipes that brought them fond memories; I wanted foods that were a part of special family and community times. Perhaps these pages also give some commentary about certain of our struggles! The tension between our love for rich, heavy foods and our concerns about short food supplies and healthful eating is evident here. That contradiction is part of our character these days. And, clearly, we don't feast all the time. This cookbook offers dishes with conscience and economy in mind, for Monday and Tuesday and February and November, as well as Saturday night and Easter!

Many of us grew up gardening and farming. What we put on our tables came from our truck patches or canning shelves. Today we are no longer bound to serve asparagus in the spring or pumpkin dishes in the fall, but few of us can deny the urge for Rhubarb Pie in May or Apple Dumplings in October. Others of us can't imagine Christmas without Peppernuts or family reunions without Burnt Sugar Cake. *The Festival Cookbook* is arranged by seasons for those reasons. (For those recipes made without any particular connection to seasons or holidays, I've included an "All Seasons" section.)

May you enjoy these recipes and the warmth that comes from sharing good food with family and friends!

—Phyllis Pellman Good

Winter

Winter and the sky falls grey. The earth turns brown and warmth moves inside.

Cold but not dead, fringed with icicles and surrounded by freezing puddles, winter overtakes the land. Family gatherings, rhythmic carols, and bells and cookies keep its frosty reaches at bay.

Fend off the blues and cabin fever with Newfoundland Soup and Apricot Sponge. Let the children press the raisins onto the Hungarian Coffee Cake.

Put together Wassail and Cranberry Christmas Pudding. There's company coming!

. . . the rain comes down, and the snow from heaven, and returns not thither, but waters the earth, and makes it bring forth and bud, that it may give seed to the sower, and bread to the eater.

—Isaiah 55:10

Christmas Breads

Sweet Dough

> *2 cups warm water*
> *2 Tbsp. dry yeast*
> *1/2 cup sugar*
> *2 tsp. salt*
> *2 eggs*
> *1/2 cup oil*
> *7-7 1/2 cups flour, sifted*

1. Dissolve yeast in water. Add sugar, salt, eggs, and oil. Mix well. Add half of flour. Beat well. Add remaining flour, using just enough to make a stiff dough. Let rest a few minutes on floured board.
2. Knead until smooth and elastic, about 5 minutes. Place in oiled bowl, cover, and let rise in warm place until doubled. Punch down and let rise again till doubled.
3. Divide for rolls or coffee cakes and shape accordingly.

Note: You can use the Sweet Dough recipe to make Tea Rings, Wreaths, Christmas Trees, French Coffee Lace, or Christmas Braid, besides Stollen and Hungarian Coffee Cake, which I have included here.

Stollen

> *1/2 of sweet dough*
> *1/2 cup almonds, cut up and blanched*
> *1/4 cup citron, cut up*
> *1/4 cup cherries, candied*
> *1 cup raisins, seeded*
> *1 Tbsp. lemon rind, grated*
> *butter, melted*

1. Flatten dough after second rising. Knead remaining ingredients into dough.
2. Pat out dough into an oval 8″x12″. Spread with butter. Fold in half the long way and shape into a crescent. Press folded edge firmly so it won't spring open. Place on lightly greased baking sheet. Brush top with butter, and let rise till doubled.
3. Bake at 350° for 35–45 minutes.
4. Frost while warm with 10X icing, and decorate with reserved pieces of almonds, citron, and cherries, if desired.

Hungarian Coffee Cake

> *½ of sweet dough*
> *½ cup butter, melted*
> *¾ cup sugar*
> *1 tsp. cinnamon*
> *½ cup nuts, finely chopped*
> *raisins (optional)*

1. After second rising of sweet dough, cut into pieces of walnut size. Form into balls.
2. Dip each ball in butter. Then roll in mixture of sugar, cinnamon, and nuts.
3. Place 1 layer of balls so they barely touch in well greased 9″ tube pan. Sprinkle with raisins, pressing them in slightly. Add another layer of balls and sprinkle with more raisins. Let rise for 45 minutes.
4. Bake at 375° for 35–40 minutes.
5. Loosen from pan. Invert pan so butter-sugar mixture runs down over cake. To serve, break apart with 2 forks.

I usually make more Christmas breads than cookies at Christmas time. It takes less time. I often give them to neighbors and friends. I also often make some for my husband to serve to his college classes the day before vacation.

—Sally Jo Milne, Goshen, Indiana

Newfoundland Christmas
Sweet Bread

Makes 4–5 loaves

> **2 pkgs. dry yeast**
> **4 cups lukewarm water**
> **2 tsp. sugar**
> **3 Tbsp. shortening, melted**
> **1 cup dark molasses**
> **6 Tbsp. sugar**
> **4 tsp. salt**
> **10–12 cups flour**
> **3 cups raisins**
> **2–3 tsp. caraway seeds, optional**

1. Dissolve yeast in 1 cup of lukewarm water to which 2 tsp. sugar have been added.
2. Combine remaining 3 cups water, shortening, molasses, sugar, and salt. Stir in dissolved yeast.
3. In large bowl measure 8 cups flour, raisins, and caraway seeds. Add liquid mixture. Stir well. Add additional flour as necessary and knead to form a soft, smooth dough.
4. Grease top of dough and cover. Let rise until double—about 2 hours. Form into loaves. Place in greased pans and let rise until double again— about 1 hour. Bake at 375° for about 60 minutes. Brush tops with melted butter.

In Newfoundland this bread is used for the Christmas Eve celebration at a thanksgiving meal.

—Verla Fae Haas, Bluesky, Alberta

Festival Prune Bread

Makes 3 (9" x 5" x 3") loaves
or 6 small loaves

>   8 cups unbleached flour
>   2¼ cups milk, scalded
>   ¼ cup shortening
>   ¼ cup sugar
>   ½ Tbsp. salt
>   2 pkgs. active dry yeast
>   ½ cup water, warmed
>   2 eggs, slightly beaten
>   2 tsp. ground cinnamon
>   2 Tbsp. fresh orange peel, grated
>   2 cups prunes, pitted and cut in fourths
>   1 cup walnuts, chopped

1. Sift and measure flour into large mixing bowl.
2. Scald milk and pour into large bowl. Add sugar, salt, and shortening. Cool until lukewarm.
3. Sprinkle yeast on warm water; stir to dissolve. Add 1 cup flour, eggs, and yeast to lukewarm milk mixture. Beat hard with spoon or mixer at medium speed for 2 minutes. Stir in cinnamon, orange peel, prunes (dusted with a little flour) and walnuts. Add remaining flour, a little at a time, until you can easily handle the soft dough.
4. Sprinkle about 2 Tbsp. flour (usually more) on board and turn out dough. Knead until dough is satiny and elastic, about 5 minutes. Shape into smooth ball and place in lightly greased bowl. Turn dough over to grease top. Cover and let rise in warm place until doubled—2½ hours. Punch down.
5. Turn dough onto board and divide according to size of baking utensil. Let rest 10 minutes. Place each portion in a well greased pan. Cover and let rise until doubled.
6. Bake at 375° until well browned, about 35–40 minutes for regular pans, 20–25 minutes for small pans.

Icing

>   2½ cups powdered sugar, sifted
>   3 Tbsp. butter, melted
>   1 Tbsp. fresh orange peel, grated

3 Tbsp. orange juice

1. Combine all ingredients.
2. Frost top of loaves when cool.

—Charlotte Rosenberger, Hatfield, Pennsylvania

Fool-Proof Bread

Makes 5 loaves

1/2 cup lukewarm water
1 tsp. sugar
2 pkgs. dry yeast
**1 qt. potato water or 1 cup mashed potatoes plus water,
   lukewarm**
1/4 cup sugar
1 Tbsp. salt
1/2 cup shortening, melted
**10–11 cups flour (3 cups whole wheat flour can be used in place of
   3 cups white flour)**
butter

1. In lukewarm water dissolve sugar and yeast. Set aside.
2. Mix together remaining ingredients except butter, adding flour a few cups at a time. Add dissolved yeast and turn out on floured board.
3. Knead at least 5 minutes.
4. Shape dough into ball and place in large, greased bowl, turning over so that top of dough is greased. Cover with towel and let rise till doubled. Punch down and let rise 1 hour.
5. Shape into 5 loaves and place in greased bread pans. Let rise till mounding over pans.
6. Bake at 375° for 30 minutes or till golden brown and loaves sound hollow when tapped.
7. Remove from pans. Butter tops.

—Mrs. David Reichenbach, Columbus Grove, Ohio

Seven Cereal Bread

Makes 3 loaves

> 2 Tbsp. dry yeast
> 1 cup warm water
> pinch sugar
> 2 cups warm water
> 1 cup buttermilk
> ½ cup molasses or brown sugar
> 1 Tbsp. salt
> 4 Tbsp. oil
> 1 cup whole wheat or rye flour
> ½ cup seven cereal flour
> ½ cup wheat germ
> 1 cup bran
> 3 cups white flour, unbleached

1. Dissolve yeast in 1 cup water and sugar. Add remaining ingredients except white flour. Mix well and let rise 30 minutes.
2. Add white flour and knead 10 minutes. Let rise 1½–2 hours.
3. Punch down and let rise 1 hour.
4. Place in 3 greased bread pans. Let rise 45 minutes.
5. Bake at 350° for 35–40 minutes.

—*Judy Classen, Newton, Kansas*

Honey Oatmeal Bread

Makes 2 loaves

> 1 cup rolled oats
> 2 cups boiling water
> 2 pkgs. dry yeast
> ⅓ cup warm water
> ½ cup honey
> 1 Tbsp. salt
> 4–6 cups flour

1. Place rolled oats in bowl. Pour boiling water over oats. Allow to cool for ¹/₂ hour.
2. Dissolve yeast in warm water.
3. Combine yeast mixture, oatmeal, honey, and salt. Measure 4 cups of flour into large bowl. Pour mixture over flour and stir. Add additional flour as necessary and knead dough until smooth.
4. Let rise until double. Divide dough in half and form loaves. Place in two greased 9" x 5" pans. Let rise again.
5. Bake at 350° for 35 minutes.

—Marilyn Forbes, Lutherville, Maryland

Spinach Bread

Makes 10–12 servings

> ¹/₄ **cup butter or margarine**
> **1 cup flour**
> **1 tsp. salt**
> **1 tsp. baking powder**
> **2 eggs**
> **1 cup milk**
> ¹/₂–³/₄ **lb. Monterey Jack or Muenster cheese, grated**
> **10-oz. pkg. spinach, thawed, chopped, and drained**

1. Preheat oven to 375°.
2. Melt butter in 9"x13" baking pan.
3. Combine all ingredients, then mix with melted butter.
4. Bake at 350° for 30–35 minutes.
5. Cool 5 minutes before cutting into squares.

—Rosetta Mast, Clarence, New York

Yeast Corn Bread

Makes 12 servings

> ³/₄ *cup water, boiling*
> ¹/₂ *cup cornmeal*
> **3 Tbsp. shortening**
> ¹/₄ *cup molasses*
> **2 tsp. salt**
> **1 pkg. dry yeast**
> ¹/₄ *cup warm water*
> **1 egg**
> **3 cups flour, sifted**

1. Pour boiling water over cornmeal, shortening, molasses and salt.
2. Dissolve yeast in warm water. Add yeast, egg, and half of the flour to cornmeal mixture. Beat 2 minutes. Add remaining flour and blend well.
3. Put in greased bread pan and let rise till double in size.
4. Bake at 375° for 50–55 minutes.

—*Sanford and Orpha Eash, Goshen, Indiana*

Canadian Bran Muffins

Makes 18–24 muffins

> ¹/₂ *cup oil*
> **1 Tbsp. dark molasses**
> **1 cup brown sugar**
> **2 cups natural bran**
> **2 cups buttermilk**
> **1 cup flour**
> **1 cup whole wheat flour**
> **2 tsp. baking soda**
> ¹/₂ *cup raisins or dates*

1. Cream together oil, molasses, and brown sugar. Gradually add bran and buttermilk.
2. Sift together flours and soda. Add raisins or dates and mix lightly. Com-

bine flour and sugar mixture. Mix just until moistened.
3. Fill greased muffin tins ¾ full. Bake at 400° for 15 minutes.

—Rita Yoder, Irwin, Pennsylvania

Oat Muffins

Makes 12–18 muffins

> **3 cups oat flakes or wheat flakes**
> **2 cups fruit juice**
> **¹/₂ cup raisins**
> **1 cup whole wheat pastry flour**
> **¹/₂ tsp. salt**
> **¹/₂ tsp. cinnamon**
> **3 Tbsp. vegetable oil**
> **1 egg, optional**
> **¹/₃ cup sunflower seeds or chopped nuts**

1. Preheat oven to 375° and insert muffin tins.
2. Stir oat flakes in a heavy dry skillet over low heat. While oats are being toasted, bring fruit juice and raisins to a boil in a saucepan.
3. Pour the oat flakes into a bowl and pour the juice and fruit over them. Let flakes sit 5 minutes to absorb liquid. Beat in remaining ingredients.
4. Remove muffin tins and brush wells with oil. Spoon batter almost to top of each well.
5. Bake for 15 minutes at 375°, then reduce heat to 350° and bake another 30 minutes.

—Elaine Good, Urbana, Illinois

Nutritious Muffins

Makes 30 muffins

> **16-oz. can evaporated milk**
> **³/₄ cup all-bran cereal**
> **¹/₂ cup rolled oats**
> **¹/₂ cup rye flakes (may substitute rolled oats)**
> **1 cup brown sugar**
> **1 cup flour**
> **¹/₄ cup whole wheat or graham flour**
> **¹/₄ cup wheat germ**
> **1 tsp. baking powder**
> **¹/₂ tsp. baking soda**
> **1³/₄ tsp. salt**
> **¹/₂ cup sunflower seeds**
> **2 cups raisins**
> **¹/₂ cup cooking oil**
> **2 large eggs, well beaten**
> **2 tsp. vanilla**
> **sesame seeds**

1. Combine milk, bran, oats, and rye. Set aside.
2. Combine sugar, flours, baking powder, baking soda, salt, sunflower seeds, and raisins.
3. Add oil, eggs, and vanilla to wet oat mixture. Pour this combination into dry ingredients and stir only until moistened.
4. Fill paper-lined muffin tins ⅞ full with batter. Sprinkle muffin tops generously with sesame seeds using at least ¼ tsp. for each muffin.
5. Bake at 350° for 20–25 minutes.

—Ellen Helmuth, Debec, New Brunswick

Quick Pecan Rolls

Makes 8 rolls

> ¹/₂ cup brown sugar
> 1 Tbsp. dark corn syrup
> ¹/₄ cup butter, melted
> ¹/₃ cup chopped pecans
> 1¹/₂ cups flour
> 2¹/₄ tsp. baking powder
> ¹/₂ tsp. salt
> 3 Tbsp. sugar
> ¹/₄ cup shortening
> 1 egg, slightly beaten
> ¹/₃ cup milk
> 1 Tbsp. butter, melted
> 2 Tbsp. sugar
> ¹/₂ tsp. cinnamon

1. Combine brown sugar, syrup, and ¹/₄ cup butter. Mix well. Divide syrup among 8 muffin cups. Sprinkle syrup with pecans divided evenly between muffin cups.
2. Combine flour, baking powder, salt, and sugar. Cut in shortening. Add egg and milk and stir just until blended. Knead in bowl 8–10 times.
3. Shape or roll dough into 8″ x 12″ rectangle. Brush with butter and sprinkle with sugar and cinnamon. Starting at short end, roll dough. Seal edges. Cut into 8 slices and place on top of syrup in each muffin cup. Bake at 375° for 20–25 minutes.

—Ruth Todd, Manheim, Pennsylvania

Clam-Shrimp Chowder

Makes 6 servings

> 2 cans cream of potato soup
> 1 can cream of shrimp soup
> 1½–2 cans milk
> 1 can clams, with juice
> 1 can tuna, with juice
> 1 can mushroom pieces, with juice
> 1 cup cheddar cheese, grated
> salt to taste
> pepper to taste
> ¼ stick butter or margarine

Heat all ingredients together slowly. Do not boil.

We celebrate "Unexpected Company" with this soup. One Sunday evening our phone rang and someone asked when our evening church service began. The caller explained that they had just talked to their preacher, who was now on his way to our house for supper. My husband, Ellis, sucked in his breath, covered the phone mouthpiece, and in a loud whisper said, "Charlotte, I forgot to tell you that I'd invited Randy and Diane and the children for supper! Do you have some soup in the freezer?"

My mind raced from the empty freezer to my stock shelves. By that time, literally, the door bell rang and the Nafzigers were there. I met them at the door with a blushing explanation that we'd forgotten they were coming, but please would they come on in, and they could help me get supper on the table.

Everyone pitched in, even the noon dinner guest who was still here. We opened cans, put leftover dessert on the table, and made a tossed salad. In just 25 minutes, with a soup tureen in the middle of the table, we had an ample, attractive meal ready to sit down to. We laughed a lot and had good fellowship.

For little fuss and lots of fun, I recommend unexpected company.

—Charlotte Croyle, Archbold, Ohio

Salmon Soup

Makes 6 servings

> **4 Tbsp. butter**
> **3 quarts milk**
> **2 cups salmon**
> **salt and pepper to taste**

1. Brown butter in kettle. Add milk and seasonings. When hot, add salmon, flaked with a fork.
2. Serve with crackers.

—Betty Pellman, Millersville, Pennsylvania

Fish Chowder

Makes 5–6 servings

> **5 slices bacon, chopped**
> **3 onions, chopped**
> **1¹/₂ lbs. cod**
> **1 pt. cream or half and half**
> **5 potatoes, cooked, peeled, and diced**
> **water, desired amount cooked with potatoes**
> **turmeric, ground**
> **salt to taste**
> **pepper to taste**

1. Sauté bacon with onions until onions are tender.
2. Cut cod in 2″ cubes. Add to sauteed onions, cooking till cod is flaky. Stir slightly.
3. Add cream. Add potatoes and water. Sprinkle with turmeric. Season.

—Joan Stroud, Pawcatuck, Connecticut

Corny Fish Chowder

Makes 6 servings

> 1 onion, chopped
> 1/4 cup butter
> 4 potatoes, cubed
> 2 tsp. salt
> 1/4 tsp. pepper
> 1/2 tsp. basil
> 3 cups water
> 1 lb. frozen cod, cut in cubes
> 1 1/2 cups frozen corn
> 13-oz. can evaporated milk

1. Sauté onion in butter till soft, but not brown. Add next 5 ingredients and simmer 15 minutes.
2. Add cod and corn. Cook 15 more minutes. Add milk; heat, but do not boil.

— *Rita Yoder, Irwin, Pennsylvania*

Chicken (or Turkey) Chowder

Makes 6–8 servings

> 1 chicken (or leftover turkey)
> 8 cups water
> 2 cups celery, leaves and all
> 1 green pepper
> 6 carrots, cubed
> 1 onion
> 2 medium apples, pared and chopped
> 4–6 Tbsp. flour
> 2 1/2 tsp. salt
> 1 Tbsp. sugar
> 1/2 tsp. curry powder
> 3 tomatoes

1. Cook chicken or turkey in water.
2. Sauté celery, green pepper, carrots, onion, and apples together for about 10 minutes. Add flour, salt, sugar, and curry powder.
3. Add vegetables to broth. Then add chicken and tomatoes. Simmer for 1 hour.

—Anna Mary Brubacher, Kitchener, Ontario

Hamburger Soup

Makes desired amount, according to amount of ingredients!

> *1/4–1/2 lb. hamburger*
> *1 onion, chopped*
> *2–3 cups water*
> *1½ cups macaroni*
> *½ tsp. salt*
> *1 can mushroom soup*
> *1¼ cups milk*

1. Fry hamburger and onion for a few minutes. Add water and bring to boil. Add macaroni and salt. Cook till macaroni is soft.
2. Add mushroom soup and milk. Heat well.

We were a family of nine and this soup could be adapted and stretched to serve any number. My father was a pastor and Saturdays were full preparing for Sunday. So Mother cooked this soup every Saturday supper.

—Wyonne Weber, Bluesky, Alberta

Rancher Stew

Makes 6 servings

> ¹/₄ cup shortening
> 1 medium onion, chopped
> 2 lbs. beef cubes or hamburger
> ¹/₄ cup flour
> 2 cups tomato juice
> ¹/₂ tsp. marjoram
> 2 tsp. salt
> 1 tsp. parsley
> 2 bay leaves
> 1 Tbsp. sugar
> ¹/₂ tsp. pepper
> 1 cup water
> 4 medium potatoes, cubed
> 4 carrots, cut in strips
> ¹/₂ cup celery, diced
> 1¹/₂ cups peas

1. Melt shortening in skillet.
2. Sauté onions and remove from skillet.
3. Dredge meat in flour and brown in skillet. Add next 8 ingredients, cooking for 1 hour or till meat is tender.
4. Add potatoes, carrots, and celery. Cook 30 more minutes before adding peas. Cook 10 more minutes. Remove bay leaves and serve.

—Bessie Nussbaum, Apple Creek, Ohio

Newfoundland Soup

Makes 15–20 servings

> 3–4 lbs. corned beef, cut in 1″ cubes
> 3–4 cups potatoes, cubed
> 2–3 cups turnips, cubed
> 1–2 cups carrots, diced
> 1 cup onions, chopped
> 2–4 cups tomatoes or tomato juice

¹/₄ *cup rice*
salt to taste

1. Place beef in large soup kettle. Add raw vegetables. Cover with water and boil. Add tomatoes, rice, and salt. Bring to a boil.
2. After soup reaches boiling point, simmer 1–2 hours till vegetables are tender. More water may be added if needed.

This is THE soup in Newfoundland. It is eaten at least once a week—huge kettles of it.

—Verla Fae Haas, Bluesky, Alberta

Lentil Sausage Soup

Makes 4 quarts

¹/₄ *lb. hot Italian sausage*
³/₄ *lb. sweet Italian sausage*
¹/₄ *cup water*
2 cups onion, chopped fine
2 garlic cloves, minced
4 carrots, sliced
³/₄ *cup celery, chopped*
¹/₄ *cup parsley sprigs, minced*
2 cups lentils, rinsed
2 cups cooked tomatoes, peeled, quartered and undrained
2¹/₂ qts. water
1¹/₂ Tbsp. salt
¹/₄ *tsp. pepper*
1 Tbsp. basil

1. In covered 8-quart saucepan, cook sausage in ¹/₄ cup water, over low heat, till water evaporates.
2. Brown sausage uncovered, then drain on paper towels. Slice ¹/₂″ thick and reserve. Pour off all but ¹/₄ cup of drippings.
3. Cook onions and garlic. Stir in remaining ingredients slowly. Boil over medium-low heat. Simmer covered for 30 minutes.
4. Stir in sausage and simmer till lentils are tender, about 20 minutes.

—Luella Gerig, Mishawaka, Indiana

Lentil Chili Con Carne

Makes 6 servings

> ¹/₂ lb. ground beef, crumbled
> 1 medium onion, chopped
> ¹/₂ green pepper, chopped
> 2 cups tomatoes, canned
> 1 Tbsp. chili powder
> 2 tsp. salt
> 2 cups water
> 1 cup lentils

1. Lightly brown beef, onion, and pepper in skillet. Pour off fat.
2. Stir in remaining ingredients. Cover and cook slowly for 45 minutes.

Lentil Chili Con Carne is a good recipe for an elementary classroom cooking project, especially during nutrition week. This dish is also a good meat stretcher.

—Ruby Lehman, Towson, Maryland

Barley Soup

Makes 8 servings

> ³/₄ cup pearl barley
> 2 cups water
> 2 qts. beef stock
> ¹/₂ cup celery, diced
> 1 cup carrots, grated
> 1 cup potatoes, grated
> salt and pepper to taste

1. Simmer barley in water until tender and water is all absorbed.
2. Combine celery, carrots, and potatoes in 1 quart beef stock and cook until tender. Add barley and seasonings.
3. Simmer several minutes and add other quart of beef stock.

—Betty Pellman, Millersville, Pennsylvania

Gritz Soup

Makes 4 servings

> **4 cups chicken broth**
> **1 egg**
> **¹/₂ cup cracked buckwheat groats or kasha**
> **parsley flakes**
> **salt to taste**
> **pepper to taste**
> **bits of cooked chicken (optional)**

1. Heat chicken broth to boiling point.
2. Crack egg into groats and beat with fork. Stir moistened groats into broth. Bring to boiling point, then simmer for 12–15 minutes.
3. Add fresh or dried parsley and season to taste. Bits of cooked chicken may be added.

For me, this recipe falls under the category of "Soul Food." The Hutterites brought it to South Dakota from Russia, I think, in the 1870s. In grocery stores in Freeman, South Dakota, one used to be able to buy "gritz" in bulk.

It is the sort of everyday recipe one can prepare in a hurry, and a good way to use up the meat picked from ribs, backs, and neck. It is often the third meal provided by one chicken.

—Marian Kleinsasser Towne, Indianapolis, Indiana

Nookala Soup (Egg Dumpling Soup)

Makes 6 servings

> **6 cups chicken broth**
> **2–3 eggs, beaten**
> **1¹/₂ cups flour**
> **¹/₂ tsp. salt**
> **¹/₄ tsp. baking powder**
> **pepper to taste**
> **parsley flakes**
> **chicken bits, cooked (optional)**

1. Bring chicken broth to boiling point.
2. Combine egg, flour, salt, and baking powder. Beat with fork. (Batter should be thick and lumpy.)
3. Moisten teaspoon in broth before dipping into batter. Drop batter by teaspoons into boiling broth. Reduce heat, cover pot, and simmer 10–15 minutes. Season with pepper and parsley flakes. Chicken bits may be added.

I learned to make this recipe as a child. It also falls under the category, "Soul Food." It is economical, easy to prepare, and cures many ills, including depression and stress! A male cousin of mine, Samuel Hofer of Morton, Illinois, makes this for his family (and guests) on Sunday evenings. It is the equivalent of Jewish Mother's Chicken Soup.

—Marian Kleinsasser Towne, Indianapolis, Indiana

Potato-Cheese Soup

Makes 4–6 servings.

> **5–6 potatoes, peeled and quartered**
> **³/₄ cup celery, diced**
> **¹/₂ sweet, white onion, chopped**
> **¹/₄ tsp. garlic salt**
> **¹/₄ tsp. pepper, freshly ground**
> **¹/₄ tsp. thyme**
> **1 qt. milk**

1 cup mild cheese, grated
butter

1. Cook first 6 ingredients in just enough water to cover. Cook till vegetables are tender.
2. Remove from stove. Mash all ingredients with potato masher.
3. Return to heat, heating slowly while stirring in milk. Add cheese. Stir till cheese is melted and soup is hot.
4. Place dollops of butter in each soup bowl before serving. Serve directly from kettle if desired. Butter melts and floats to top and looks great!

Note: Florets of broccoli can be added with cheese for flavor and color.

There is nothing like hot soup after raking leaves or a walk in the snow, or before bundling up to go to a soccer game. John and I both work, so at least once a week we invite someone to "come along home—we're having soup!"

—**Naomi Lederach, Hesston, Kansas**

Cream of Corn Chowder

Makes 4 servings

2 slices bacon, chopped
1 onion, chopped
2 cups milk
1 pt. creamed corn
1/2 tsp. salt
dash pepper
1 cup potatoes, diced and cooked
croutons
parsley, chopped fine

1. In large pot sauté the chopped bacon and onion very gently, stirring constantly until onions are limp. (Neither bacon nor onion should be browned at all or it will spoil the color of the finished soup.)
2. Add milk, corn, salt, pepper, and prepared potatoes. Bring to simmering point.
3. Serve topped with croutons and parsley.

—**Madeline Roth, London, Ontario**

Borscht

3 cups cabbage, grated
3 carrots, grated
1 onion, chopped
3 potatoes, grated
4 beef bouillon cubes
3 cups stewed tomatoes
1 sprig parsley
1 bay leaf
salt to taste
pepper to taste
1 sprig dill
6 cups water

Simmer all ingredients in large kettle for 30 minutes.
Note: 1 teaspoon of thick sour cream may be added to each bowl of soup if desired.

This soup gets better with every reheating. It is just a good hot soup for lunch on any cool day.

—Elfrieda and Peter Dyck, Akron, Pennsylvania

Savoy Cabbage Soup

Makes 6 servings

3 Tbsp. butter or margarine
1 onion, chopped fine
¼ cup rice, uncooked
3–4 cups cabbage, coarsely shredded
2 cups beef, cooked and cubed
6–8 cups beef broth
salt to taste
pepper to taste
cheese, grated (optional)

1. Melt butter in large kettle. Add onion and cook till light brown. Add rice and cook 1 minute, stirring constantly. Add cabbage and cook for

several minutes. Add beef and broth. Add salt and pepper. Simmer till rice is well cooked.
2. Serve with grated cheese in a side dish.

—Lena Wenger, Green Bay, Wisconsin

Cranberry Salad

Makes 6–8 servings

3-oz. pkg. raspberry gelatin
1 cup water, boiling
16-oz. can whole-berry cranberry sauce
8 oz. sour cream
¹/₂ cup nutmeats, chopped

1. Dissolve gelatin in water. Stir in cranberry sauce. Cool until syrupy consistency.
2. Add sour cream and nutmeats. Mix well and chill until set.

—Rachel Wyse, Bloomfield, Iowa

Cranberry Relish

Makes 10–12 servings

1 lb. raw cranberries
3 apples, cored
3 oranges
8¹/₂-oz. can pineapple, crushed and undrained
1¹/₂ cups sugar

1. Grind cranberries, apples, and oranges. Add pineapple and sugar. Mix well.
2. Refrigerate 12–24 hours before serving.

—Elizabeth Frank, East Petersburg, Pennsylvania

Holiday Gelatin Salad

Makes 12 servings

> 2 3-oz. pkgs. red gelatin
> 3 cups water, boiling
> 3 apples, cored
> 2 oranges, whole
> 1/2 lb. raw cranberries
> 1 cup carrots, grated
> 1 cup nutmeats, cut up
> 2 cups sugar

1. Dissolve gelatin in water. Set aside till consistency of egg whites.
2. Cut apples and oranges in sections. Put through food chopper. Put cranberries through food chopper. Add carrots, nuts, and sugar. Stir well.
3. As gelatin starts to set, add fruit mixture. Pour into lightly greased molds. Chill 4–6 hours.
4. Unmold on bed of salad greens. Serve with a dressing, made the day before.

Dressing

> *miniature marshmallows*
> *sour cream*
> *mayonnaise*

Mix together all ingredients of equal amounts as much as desired.

—Phyllis Eller, LaVerne, California

Green Beans Supreme

Makes 4 servings

> 2 pkgs. frozen French style green beans (or equal amount canned or fresh beans)
> 1/3–1/2 cup onion, chopped
> 1/3–1/2 cup green pepper, chopped
> 2 Tbsp. butter or margarine

2 Tbsp. flour
½ tsp. salt
¼ tsp. pepper
1 cup sour cream
½ cup sharp cheddar cheese, shredded

1. Cook green beans until soft.
2. Melt butter in large skillet. Sauté onion and peppers. Add flour, salt and pepper and mix. Add sour cream and heat. Blend in cooked green beans. Pour into shallow 1-quart baking dish. Top with cheese. Sprinkle with paprika.
3. Bake for 15 minutes at 350°.

—Mildred Miller, Bronx, New York

Cabbage, Carrots and Onions

Makes 6 servings

½ head cabbage, chopped in thin slices
3 medium-sized carrots, sliced thin
1 large onion, sliced thin
4 Tbsp. margarine

1. Layer vegetables into heavy saucepan in order given.
2. Top with slices of margarine.
3. Steam gently over low heat until vegetables are tender and margarine has melted.
4. Invert cooked vegetables into serving dish.

Note: This dish needs no seasoning or water for cooking. The natural moisture of the vegetables will steam them.

This is like eating pure health!

—Merle Good, Lancaster, Pennsylvania

Brandywine Scalloped Potatoes

Makes 6–8 servings

> **6 large potatoes, cooked**
> **salt to taste**
> **pepper to taste**
> **1 cup longhorn or colby cheese, grated**
> **2 Tbsp. butter or margarine**
> **1¹/₂–2 cups milk**

1. Skin and grate cooled potatoes.
2. Place a layer of potatoes into an oblong, greased 8″ x 14″ baking dish. Add seasonings and half the cheese. Add a second layer of potatoes and seasonings. Dot with butter. Add milk and rest of cheese.
3. Bake at 350° for 35–40 minutes or until it is hot throughout and cheese is melted.

—Miriam Weaver, Harrisonburg, Virginia

Mashed Spinach Potatoes

Makes 6–8 servings

> **6–8 potatoes, cooked and mashed**
> **³/₄ cup sour cream**
> **1 tsp. sugar**
> **¹/₄ lb. butter or margarine, softened**
> **2 tsp. salt**
> **¹/₄ tsp. pepper**
> **2 Tbsp. chives, chopped**
> **¹/₄ tsp. dill leaves**
> **1 pkg. spinach, cooked and drained**
> **1 cup cheddar cheese, shredded**

1. Combine first 6 ingredients. Beat until light and fluffy. Add chives, dill and spinach. Place in baking dish and sprinkle with cheese.
2. Bake at 400° for 20 minutes.

—Doris Miller, Kidron, Ohio

Scalloped Squash with Apples

Makes 6 servings

> **2 cups squash, cooked, drained and cut up**
> **2 cups apple slices**
> **¼ cup brown sugar**
> **2 tsp. lemon juice**
> **½ tsp. nutmeg or allspice**
> **4 Tbsp. butter, melted**

1. Arrange squash and apples in layers in buttered baking dish, saving 1 layer of squash for the very top. Sprinkle with sugar, lemon juice, and spices. Add last layer of squash. Pour butter over top.
2. Bake at 375° for 30 minutes.

Note: Sweet potatoes may be substituted for squash.

If casserole seems dry, pour on water, orange juice, or juice drained from the squash.

—Lena Wenger, Green Bay, Wisconsin

Baked Barley Casserole

Makes 2–3 servings

> **1 onion, chopped**
> **¼ cup butter or margarine**
> **½ cup raw barley**
> **½ cup mushrooms, sliced**
> **2 cups chicken broth**

1. Sauté onion in butter.
2. Mix with remaining ingredients. Pour into 9″ x 9″ baking dish and cover.
3. Bake at 325° for 2 hours, stirring after 1 hour.

Note: For variations add cooked chicken or turkey before baking.

—Ginny Birky, Cortez, Colorado

Zucchini Delight

Makes 6 servings

> 1/4 lb. hamburger or cubed steak
> 2–3 onions, diced
> 4–5 young squash
> 4 tomatoes
> 1 tsp. salt
> dash pepper
> dash marjoram
> dash basil
> 3–4 slices cheddar cheese

1. Braise meat and onions over low heat. Add squash, tomatoes and seasonings.
2. Simmer over low heat, covered, stirring occasionally until squash is tender.
3. Lay cheese slices over top and serve.

This is an original Brubaker dish!

—Kenton Brubaker, Harrisonburg, Virginia

Farmers Vegetable Omelet

Makes 2 servings

> 5 eggs
> 1/4–1/2 cup milk
> 1 onion, chopped
> 1/2 cup celery, chopped
> 1 garlic clove, minced
> 2–3 cups assorted raw vegetables, chopped or grated
> cheese, grated
> salt to taste
> pepper to taste

1. Beat eggs with milk.

2. Sauté vegetables and garlic in oil till almost cooked (5–10 minutes). Stir in eggs.
3. Sprinkle with cheese, salt, and pepper, frying omelet till set.

—Susan Davis, Nashville, Tennessee

Potato Omelet

Makes 6 servings

> ¹/₂ *cup onion, chopped fine*
> ¹/₂ *cup green peppers, chopped fine*
> ¹/₂ *lb. bacon*
> *6 potatoes, peeled and grated*
> *6 eggs, beaten*
> *salt to taste*
> *pepper to taste*
> *1 cup cheese, grated*

1. Sauté the chopped onions and pepper in a little butter until tender. Set aside.
2. Brown bacon until crisp. Drain and cool.
3. Brown grated potatoes until cooked. Add sautéed onion and pepper by folding in gently. Pour beaten eggs over potato, onion, and pepper mixture which has been seasoned to taste with salt and pepper.
4. Sprinkle top with grated cheese and crumbled bacon.
5. Cover the skillet and let omelet cook over low heat, or layer mixture in a baking dish and bake at 325° until set.

—Edna Brunk, Upper Marlboro, Maryland

Egg and Cheese Bake

Makes 8–12 servings

> *³/₄ cup butter*
> *1 cup biscuit mix*
> *1¹/₂ cups cottage cheese*
> *¹/₂ lb. cheddar cheese, grated*
> *2 tsp. onion, diced*
> *1 tsp. parsley flakes*
> *¹/₄ tsp. salt*
> *6 eggs, lightly beaten*
> *1 cup milk*

1. Melt butter in 13″ x 9″ x 2″ baking dish in oven.
2. Mix remaining ingredients together in order given. Pour mixture evenly over melted butter.
3. Bake at 350° for 40 minutes.

—Ruth Todd, Manheim, Pennsylvania

Chiles Rellenos José

Makes 6–8 servings

> *8-oz. can whole green chiles*
> *1 lb. Monterey Jack cheese, cut in strips 1″ wide, 3″ long, ¹/₄″ thick*
> *4 large eggs*
> *¹/₄ cup flour*
> *1¹/₄ cups milk*
> *¹/₂ tsp. salt*
> *black pepper to taste*
> *liquid red pepper to taste*
> *¹/₂ lb. cheddar cheese, grated*
> *paprika*

1. Rinse seeds from chiles. Spread in single layer on paper toweling. Carefully pat dry with more toweling. Split and insert piece of cheese.
2. Beat eggs. Gradually add flour, beating until smooth. Add milk, salt and

peppers. Beat thoroughly.

3. Arrange stuffed chiles in shallow 9″ x 13″ glass baking dish. Sprinkle with cheddar cheese and paprika. Carefully pour egg mixture over all.
4. Bake uncovered for 45 minutes at 350°.

—*Zelda Yoder, Walsenburg, Colorado*

Sandwich Spread

Makes 1¹/₂ pints of spread

> 1 lb. bacon, fried and cut up
> 1 medium onion, chopped
> 1 green pepper, chopped
> 4 stalks celery, chopped
> 1 lb. mild cheddar cheese, grated
> 10-oz. can tomato soup

1. Cook first 4 ingredients together until vegetables are tender. Remove from heat and add cheese and soup. Mix well.
2. Spread on buns or bread. Broil sandwiches.

—**Anne Loewen, Altona, Manitoba**

Chiliburgers

Makes 6–9 servings

> **1 lb. ground beef**
> **10½-oz. can condensed bean with bacon soup**
> **½ cup ketchup**
> **1 tsp. chili powder**
> **6 buns, split and toasted**

1. Brown beef in skillet.
2. Add soup, ketchup, and chili powder. Simmer 5 minutes to blend flavors, stirring often. Add water if desired.
3. Serve on buns.

A simple, fast, tasty camping dish.

—Janet Yoder, Phoenix, Arizona

Favorite Wintertime Dinner

> **1 lb. ground beef**
> **½ onion, chopped**
> **3 large potatoes**
> **3 carrots**
> **2 Tbsp. rice**
> **1 can tomato soup**
> **1½ cups tomato juice**
> **salt**
> **pepper**

1. Brown ground beef and onion. Drain off excess fat.
2. Slice potatoes and carrots thinly on vegetable grater.
3. Place in layers in large buttered casserole: half the potatoes, half the carrots, half the hamburger mixture. Cover with rice. Then place the remaining vegetables and meat in layers in the casserole. Season with salt and pepper.
4. Spread tomato soup over top. Slowly add tomato juice.

5. Cover and bake at 325° for 2 hours.

My mother, Lorene Good, usually put this dish in the oven on winter Sunday mornings before church. The oven heated the house, and at that time of the year we had plenty of carrots and potatoes. Lunch was ready when we all got home!

—Elaine Good, Urbana, Illinois

Cracked Wheat-Ground Beef Casserole

Makes 6–8 servings

> 1 lb. lean ground beef
> 1 cup celery, chopped
> 1 large green pepper, chopped
> 1 medium onion, chopped
> 1 clove garlic, minced
> 1 tsp. salt
> 1/8 tsp. pepper
> 2 cups tomatoes, cut up
> 1 cup cracked wheat
> 1 cup water
> 1/2 cup raisins
> 1/3 cup shelled sunflower seeds
> cheddar cheese, sliced and halved diagonally (optional)

1. In skillet cook ground beef, celery, green pepper, onion, garlic, salt, and pepper until meat is browned and vegetables are crisp-tender. Drain off excess fat.
2. Stir in undrained tomatoes, cracked wheat, water, raisins, and sunflower seeds. Turn mixture into a 2-qt., greased casserole dish.
3. Bake, covered, at 375° for 35 minutes or until wheat is tender.
4. If desired, uncover and top with cheese during the last 5 minutes of baking.

Note: This hearty, stick-to-the-ribs meal freezes well. I have also put it in a slow-cooker instead of a casserole to take it to pot-luck dinners. When I use a slow-cooker, I add the cheese during the last few minutes to melt it.

—Anna Ruth Beck, Halstead, Kansas

Skillet Beef Macaroni

Makes 6 servings

> 1 lb. ground beef
> 1¹/₂ cups uncooked elbow macaroni
> small onion, cut up
> green pepper, cut up (optional)
> 1 tsp. salt
> 1¹/₂ cups hot water
> 1 cube beef bouillon
> 1 Tbsp. flour
> ¹/₄ lb. cheddar cheese, cubed
> 1²/₃ cups evaporated milk

1. Brown beef, macaroni, onion and pepper. Add salt, hot water and bouillon. Cover and simmer until macaroni is cooked.
2. Sprinkle flour over the cooked mixture. Add cheese and evaporated milk. Cover and warm till cheese is melted. Stir and serve.

—Mary Glick, Goshen, Indiana

Potato Beef Casserole

Makes 8 servings

> 1 lb. ground beef
> 1 onion, chopped
> 2 cups noodles, dry
> 7 potatoes, peeled and sliced thin
> 1 cup peas or beans, frozen
> seasoning, of your choice
> 2¹/₂ cups milk
> 1 can cream of mushroom soup
> cheese slices (optional)

1. Brown beef and onion.
2. Cook noodles 5 minutes.
3. In greased baking dish, alternately layer potatoes, peas, seasonings,

beef, and noodles. Top with milk, soup, and cheese.
4. Cover, slightly open, and bake at 350° for 1 hour.

—Leora Gerber, Dalton, Ohio

Southwest Strata

Makes 8 servings

> **6 flour tortillas**
> **2 Tbsp. margarine**
> **1 cup onion, chopped**
> **1 garlic clove, crushed**
> **1 tsp. oregano**
> **¹/₂ tsp. ground cumin**
> **2 cups kidney beans, drained**
> **¹/₂ cup ripe olives, sliced**
> **4-oz. jar pimento pieces, drained**
> **4-oz. can green chiles, chopped**
> **1¹/₂ cups cheese, shredded**
> **4 eggs**
> **2 cups milk**

1. Cut tortillas into halves. Arrange half of them, overlapping, in a greased 12" x 8" x 2" baking dish.
2. Melt margarine in skillet over medium heat. Add onion, garlic, oregano, and cumin. Cook, stirring occasionally, for 2–3 minutes. Remove from heat.
3. Stir in kidney beans, olives, pimento, and chiles.
4. Spoon half the mixture over the tortillas. Sprinkle with half the cheese.
5. Add remaining tortilla pieces, bean mixture, and cheese.
6. Beat eggs and milk together. Pour evenly over cheese.
7. Bake at 350° for 40 minutes, until puffed and golden brown. Let stand 10 minutes before serving.

This meatless dish makes a hot light lunch or dinner in cold weather.

—Gloria L. Lehman, Blacksburg, Virginia

Pastitsio

Makes 12–15 servings

Meat Layer

> 1 Tbsp. butter
> 1 medium onion, chopped
> 3 lbs. ground beef
> 6-oz. can tomato paste
> 3/4 cup water
> 1 1/2 tsp. salt
> 1/4 tsp. pepper
> 2 Tbsp. allspice
> 1 tsp. nutmeg
> 1 tsp. cinnamon
> 2 eggs

1. Heat butter. Sauté onion. Add meat and fry till pink is gone. Stir in tomato paste, water, salt, pepper and spices. Cover and simmer for 5 minutes. Uncover and simmer 5 more minutes. Remove from heat.
2. Adjust salt to taste. Refrigerate. When cool, remove congealed fat. Mix in eggs and set aside.

Macaroni Layer

> 1 lb. macaroni
> 2 eggs, well beaten
> 1 cup parmesan cheese, grated
> 1/2 cup butter

1. Cook and drain macaroni. Put half in bowl. Add eggs and mix thoroughly. Spread in 11" x 14" x 2" baking pan. Sprinkle with 1/2 cup parmesan cheese.
2. Spread meat mixture over macaroni. Arrange remaining macaroni over meat layer. Sprinkle with remaining parmesan cheese.
3. Melt butter and pour over parmesan layer. Top with cream sauce.

Cream Sauce Layer

> 4 eggs
> 3/4 cup milk

1 cup parmesan cheese, grated
1 Tbsp. flour
1/2 tsp. salt
nutmeg

1. Beat eggs to a froth. Blend in cheese, milk, flour and salt. Pour over meat-macaroni layers. Sprinkle lightly with nutmeg. Cover with foil.
2. Bake in 400° oven for 15 minutes. Remove foil. Bake 30 minutes longer or until golden brown. Remove from oven. Wait 15 minutes before cutting.

My son John takes a meal-sized, foil-wrapped, prepared frozen pastitsio to graduate school. Makes bachelor cooking easier.

—Frieda Barkman, Twentynine Palms, California

Bavarian Meatballs

Makes 6–8 servings

2 lb. ground chuck
1²/₃ cups ketchup
1 can ginger ale

1. Form ground chuck into small meatballs, about the size of a quarter.
2. Place in electric fry pan and brown lightly. Add ketchup and ginger ale. Boil 1 hour at 275° or at a simmer.

—Joyce Hedrick, Lederach, Pennsylvania

East African Beef Curry

Makes 6–8 servings

> 1½ Tbsp. oil
> 1 medium onion, diced
> 2–3 Tbsp. curry powder
> 1½ lb. lean beef, cubed
> ⅓ cup mushrooms, chopped
> 1 tomato, diced
> 1 large garlic clove, minced
> 2 tsp. salt
> 2 tsp. sugar
> 2 cups (more or less) water
> 2 Tbsp. cornstarch
> 2 Tbsp. water
> 3 cups rice, cooked

1. Heat oil in heavy skillet. Sauté onion till tender.
2. Stir in curry powder and cook 1 minute. Add beef cubes, mushrooms, tomato, garlic, salt, and sugar in order given. Continue cooking till beef cubes are lightly browned. Add enough boiling water to barely cover beef. Cover and simmer for 1½–2 hours.
3. Combine cornstarch and water. Add to skillet. Heat until thickened.
4. Serve with rice and several of the following condiments.

Condiments

> onion, diced
> tomatoes, diced
> peanuts, salted
> hard-boiled eggs, diced
> cauliflower, chopped
> oranges, diced
> pickle relish
> chutney
> raisins
> dates, chopped

> bananas, diced
> green peppers, diced
> coconut, shredded
> cabbage, shredded
> cucumbers, diced
> pineapple, diced
> carrots, shredded
> apples, diced
> cheese, grated

1. Prepare condiments before serving.
2. Place in individual dishes in center of table, allowing each person to

choose what to sprinkle on top of curry and over rice.
Note: Use flank steak, stew meat, or chuck roast.

This recipe can be made a day or two ahead of time, as long as it is refrigerated, as the curry spice and other flavors steep well. It is a great socializing meal.

—Joyce Hedrick, Lederach, Pennsylvania

Pepper Steak

Makes 4–6 servings

> **1¹/₂ lbs. top sirloin, 1″ thick**
> **¹/₄ cup oil**
> **1 garlic clove, crushed**
> **¹/₂ tsp. ginger**
> **1 tsp. salt**
> **¹/₄ tsp. pepper**
> **2 green peppers, sliced**
> **2 large onions, thinly sliced**
> **¹/₄ cup soy sauce**
> **¹/₂ tsp. sugar**
> **1 cup beef bouillon**
> **8-oz. can water chestnuts, sliced**
> **4 green onions, cut in ¹/₂″ pieces**
> **2 Tbsp. cornstarch**
> **¹/₄ cup cold water**
> **2 firm tomatoes, peeled and cut into eighths**
> **rice, hot and cooked**

1. Freeze steak for at least 1 hour. When ready to cook, cut meat into ¹/₈″ thick slices.
2. Heat oil in skillet. Add garlic, ginger, salt, and pepper. Sauté till garlic is golden. Add steak and brown lightly. Remove meat. Add green peppers and onions. Cook 7–10 minutes. Return beef to pan. Add soy sauce, sugar, bouillon, water chestnuts, green onions, and cornstarch dissolved in ¹/₄ cup water. Simmer 3 minutes or until sauce thickens.
3. Add tomatoes and heat. Serve over hot rice.

—Robert Regier, North Newton, Kansas

Perishky and Sausage Rolls

Pastry Dough

> *3–3¹/₂ cups flour*
> *1 cup butter or margarine*
> *1 tsp. cream of tartar*
> *¹/₂ tsp. salt*
> *¹/₂ tsp. baking soda*

Mix as for pie crust, adding enough water to make a soft dough.

Fruit Perishky

> *pastry dough*
> *fruit of your choice, enough to fill pastry dough squares*
> *sugar*
> *flour*

1. Roll dough out as thin as desired. Cut into squares of desired size.
2. Place fruit on center of squares, sprinkling fruit with sugar and flour. Fold corners over and seal.
3. Bake at 400° for 12–15 minutes.

Sausage Rolls

> *pastry dough*
> *sausage pieces, pre-cooked, enough to fill pastry dough squares*

1. Roll out dough as thin as desired. Cut into squares of desired size.
2. Place sausage pieces on center of squares. Fold corners over and seal.
3. Bake at 400° for 12–15 minutes.

Meat Perishky

> *1 onion, chopped*
> *¹/₂ lb. ground beef*
> *1 cup potatoes, mashed*
> *¹/₂ tsp. salt*
> *pepper to taste*
> *pastry dough*

1. Sauté onions till pale yellow. Add beef and continue to brown. Add remaining ingredients except dough.
2. Roll out dough as thin as desired. Cut into squares of desired size.
3. Place beef filling on center of squares. Fold corners over and seal.
4. Bake at 400° for 12–15 minutes.

—*Anne Braun, Plum Coulee, Manitoba*

Sausage Souffle

Makes 6 servings

> **1 lb. bulk sausage**
> **6 eggs, beaten**
> **1 tsp. dry mustard**
> **1 tsp. salt**
> **2 cups milk**
> **¹/₄ lb. mild cheddar cheese, grated**
> **6 slices bread, cubed**

1. Brown sausage and drain.
2. Combine next 4 ingredients. Add sausage and cheese.
3. Place bread cubes in 9″ x 9″ baking dish. Pour mixture into dish, over crumbs.
4. Refrigerate overnight.
5. Bake at 350° for 45 minutes.

Note: Chipped or cubed ham can be substituted for sausage.

The dish may be topped with 3 cups crushed corn flakes, mixed with ¹/₂ cup melted butter.

We like this for our breakfast on Christmas morning. I make it the day before and it bakes while we open our gifts. It's then ready with no fuss from me.

—*Gladys Stoesz, Akron, Pennsylvania*

Sausage Corn Casserole

Makes 6 servings

> 4 eggs, well beaten
> 1 qt. frozen or fresh corn, cooked and drained
> 1 cup soft bread crumbs
> 1 lb. loose sausage meat, browned
> 1 tsp. salt
> 1 Tbsp. onion, chopped
> ketchup

1. Mix together all ingredients except ketchup. Pour into a deep greased casserole.
2. Spread ketchup over top.
3. Set casserole in pan of water that is 1″ deep. Bake at 350° for 1 hour.

I often make this on cold winter evenings.

—Jean Shenk, Mt. Joy, Pennsylvania

Bubaht

Makes 6 servings

> 1 Tbsp. yeast
> 1½ cups milk
> 2 Tbsp. sugar
> 2½ cups flour
> 1 tsp. salt
> 2 eggs, beaten
> 1 lb. ham or sausage (smoked)

1. Dissolve yeast in warm milk with sugar. When foamy add flour, salt and eggs.
2. Grease 2″ x 6″ x 9″ baking pan. Pour thin layer in pan. Add sausage cut in small pieces or pieces of ham. Add rest of dough; let rise again.
3. Bake 30 minutes at 375°.

—Marie Wiens, Hillsboro, Kansas

Ham Balls

Makes 10–12 servings

>   2 *lbs. ground ham*
>   2 *lbs. ground pork*
>   2 *cups corn flake crumbs*
>   2 *cups milk*
>   2 *Tbsp. dry mustard*
>   4 *eggs*

Mix well and shape into 30–35 balls (⅓ cup each).

Glaze

>   2 *cups brown sugar*
>   2 *Tbsp. dry mustard*
>   ½ *cup vinegar*

1. Heat ingredients and pour over meatballs.
2. Cover and bake at 350° for 1 hour.

—Verna Nissley, Elizabethtown, Pennsylvania

Ham 'N Apple Cheese Pie

Makes 8 servings

> **1¹/₂–2 lbs. ham slices, ¹/₂–³/₄" thick**
> **2–3 tart apples, pared and sliced**
> **¹/₃ cup flour**
> **¹/₂ cup brown sugar**
> **2 Tbsp. margarine, melted**
> **6 slices mild cheese**
> **1 cup cultured sour cream**

1. Cut ham slices into serving pieces and arrange them to cover the bottom of a greased low casserole or pie plate.
2. Arrange apple slices to cover ham.
3. Mix together the flour, brown sugar, and margarine, then crumble over apples.
4. Top with cheese slices. Drop dollops of sour cream over cheese.
5. Bake at 350° for 1 hour.

I love the mix of tastes. It seems traditional and novel at the same instant. And scrumptious!

—Merle Good, Lancaster, Pennsylvania

Chicken Broccoli Casserole

Makes 6 servings

> **10 oz. broccoli, cooked and drained**
> **1 chicken, cooked and cubed**
> **3 Tbsp. butter or margarine**
> **¹/₂ cup flour**
> **1¹/₂ cups water or chicken broth**
> **3 chicken bouillon cubes**
> **¹/₂ cup milk**
> **¹/₂ lb. cheese, grated (optional)**
> **¹/₂ cup mushrooms, sliced**
> **³/₄–1 cup bread cubes**

¹/₂ cup milk
paprika

1. Place split broccoli spears lengthwise in baking dish. Cover with chicken.
2. Combine next 6 ingredients to make sauce. Pour over chicken and sprinkle mushrooms over sauce.
3. Soak bread crumbs in ¹/₂ cup milk and add to casserole. Sprinkle with paprika.
4. Bake at 350° for 30 minutes.

—Fern Massanari, Fisher, Illinois
—Anna Bishop, Harrisonburg, Virginia

Chicken Cacciatore

Makes 6 servings

> *3 lbs. chicken, cut up*
> *paprika*
> *rosemary*
> *oregano*
> *salt to taste*
> *2 green peppers, thinly sliced*
> *2 medium onions, thinly sliced*
> *¹/₂ lb. fresh mushrooms, sliced*
> *1 can black olives, pitted and drained*
> *1 cup tomato sauce*
> *3 cups stewed tomatoes, seasoned lightly with basil*
> *6-oz. can tomato paste*
> *pinch saffron*
> *1 tsp. salt*
> *¹/₄ tsp. pepper, freshly ground*

1. Coat chicken with paprika, rosemary, and oregano. Sprinkle on salt. Bake at 350° for 1¹/₂ hours. (Bake uncovered for thin, crispy skin.)
2. Sauté peppers, onions, and mushrooms in hot oil in skillet. Add remaining ingredients. Add chicken.
3. Cover and simmer 1 hour to blend seasonings.

—Mary Ellen Miller, Sarasota, Florida

Arroz con Pollo
(Puerto Rican Rice and Chicken)

Makes 8 servings

> 2 strips bacon, cut up
> 1/4 cup ham, chopped (optional)
> 2 Tbsp. parsley, chopped
> 1 small onion, chopped
> 1 clove garlic, mashed
> 1 green pepper, chopped
> 2 cups rice, uncooked
> 3 1/3 cups chicken broth
> 2 cups chicken, cooked and cut up
> 1 cup tomato sauce
> 1/2 cup green olives
> 1 cup peas, canned or thawed

1. Fry first 6 ingredients together till onion is soft. Add rice, stirring well to coat rice with fat. Add broth and cook slowly for 15–20 minutes.
2. Add chicken and tomato sauce. Heat.
3. When ready to serve, toss in olives and peas.
Note: Don't stir more often than necessary.

Arroz Con Pollo is a recipe that my mother brought back with her after she and father worked in Puerto Rico under the Mennonite Central Committee. It was always a special dish for our family because of the stories they told along with it.

—Jan Hertzler Buerge, Kansas City, Kansas

Chicken with Orange Sauce

Makes 6–8 servings

> 1 fryer, cut up
> 2 Tbsp. oil
> salt to taste
> pepper to taste

6–8 potatoes, washed and cut up
1 cup orange juice
¼ cup brown sugar
1 tsp. ginger, ground

1. Brown chicken in hot oil. Add salt, pepper and potatoes.
2. Mix remaining ingredients and pour over chicken, coating well. Simmer 45 minutes.

—Jessie Hostetler, Portland, Oregon

Roast Wild Goose

Makes 6–8 servings

> **4 small onions**
> **2 cups orange juice**
> **½ cup sugar**
> **1 tsp. garlic powder**
> **pepper**
> **wild goose (or 2 wild ducks)**

1. Slice onions and break slices into rings. Loosely stuff bird with the onion rings. Mix dry ingredients and rub into skin of bird, saving a little aside. Pour 1 cup orange juice over bird and sprinkle on remaining dry mixture. Cover with aluminum foil and bake at 450° for 20 minutes.
2. Turn oven down to 350° and add remaining orange juice, basting bird in the juice several times. Cook at least 1 hour more (perhaps 1½–2 hours if bird is particularly large or tough), continuing to baste. Remove foil when near completion.

Note: This recipe completely camouflages the wild flavor of the birds and makes excellent gravy stock. (Delicious when served over wild rice.) When using 2 ducks instead of goose, bake at 350° for only 45 minutes (after adjusting the oven from 450°).

—Cathy Middleton, Chestertown, Maryland

Tuna in a Shell

Makes 4 servings

> **6-oz. can tuna, drained**
> **¹/₂ cup cheddar cheese, shredded**
> **¹/₂ cup celery, finely chopped**
> **¹/₄ cup onion, finely chopped**
> **¹/₄ cup salad dressing or mayonnaise**
> **2 Tbsp. pimento, chopped**
> **1 tsp. chives, chopped**
> **1 tsp. lemon juice**
> **¹/₂ tsp. salt**
> **dash pepper**
> **2 Tbsp. dry bread crumbs**
> **small pieces butter**

1. Mix all ingredients (except last two) together well. Divide into 4, ¹/₂-cup baking shells or small casseroles. Sprinkle bread crumbs on top and dot with butter.
2. Bake at 350° for 15 minutes or microwave 4–5 minutes on high.

— Jan Hertzler Buerge, Kansas City, Kansas

Scalloped Oysters

Makes 6 servings

> **3 dozen medium oysters (2¹/₂ cups) with their liquor**
> **1 cup fresh bread crumbs**
> **¹/₂ tsp. salt**
> **dash freshly ground pepper**
> **¹/₂ cup melted butter**
> **2 cups small oyster crackers**
> **1 cup heavy cream**

1. Check oysters for tiny bits of shell. Line a buttered 1¹/₂ qt. casserole with ¹/₄ cup bread crumbs. Add half the oysters and sprinkle with salt and pepper. Add ¹/₂ cup bread crumbs, ¹/₄ cup butter, oyster crackers, cream and

liquor from oysters. Add remaining oysters; sprinkle with remaining bread crumbs and butter.
2. Bake at 375° for 35 minutes.

—Mrs. Isaac Good, Denver, Pennsylvania

Buttermilk Pie

Makes 1 pie

1 egg, beaten
¹/₂ cup sugar
1 Tbsp. butter
¹/₂ tsp. baking soda
1 Tbsp. flour
1 cup buttermilk
¹/₄ tsp. vanilla
1 pie shell, unbaked

1. Cream egg, sugar and butter.
2. Mix baking soda with flour. Add to creamed mixture. Add buttermilk and vanilla.
3. Pour into crust and bake at 350° for 35 minutes.

—Violet Good, Petersburg, Ontario

Pecan Pie

Makes 6–10 servings

> ⅓ **cup butter**
> ½ **cup brown sugar**
> ½ **cup milk**
> **3 eggs, beaten**
> **1 cup light Karo® syrup**
> ½ **tsp. salt**
> ½ **tsp. vanilla**
> **1 cup pecans**
> **9″ pie shell, unbaked**

1. Cream butter and brown sugar. Blend in remaining ingredients. Pour into pie shell.
2. Bake at 350° for 1 hour.

—Lois Herr, Quarryville, Pennsylvania

Dark Blonde Fruit Cake

Makes 5 pounds

> ½ **lb. butter (no substitute)**
> **1 cup sugar**
> **5 eggs**
> 1¾ **cups flour**
> ½ **tsp. baking powder**
> ½ **tsp. salt**
> ¾ **lb. glacéd cherries (red and green), chopped in halves**
> **1 lb. candied pineapples, chopped fine**
> **4 cups pecans, coarsely chopped**
> **1 Tbsp. vanilla**
> **1 Tbsp. lemon flavor**

1. Cream butter and sugar. Beat in eggs one at a time.
2. Combine flour, baking powder and salt.
3. Mix ½ cup of flour mixture with fruits and nuts.

4. Stir remaining flour mixture into egg mixture. Blend well. Stir in vanilla and lemon flavor. Add fruit mixture. Mix well.
5. Turn into loaf pans lined with wax paper. Do not pre-heat oven. Put a shallow pan of water below cakes.
6. Bake at 325° for 3 hours or until done. Cool.

Note: I often make these as cupcakes or in small loaf pans. They can also be baked in fruit juice cans.

This is my prize Christmas cake. I have made it for 28 years. It's an old Canadian recipe I received from my mother-in-law 28 years ago.

—Ruth Rudy, La Junta, Colorado

Date and Nut Cake

Makes 15 servings

> *1 tsp. baking soda*
> *1 cup dates, chopped*
> *1 cup water, boiling*
> *2 Tbsp. butter*
> *1 egg*
> *1 cup sugar*
> *1½ cups flour, sifted*
> *1 cup walnuts, chopped*
> *1 tsp. vanilla*

1. Sprinkle baking soda over dates. Add water. Let cool.
2. Cream butter, egg and sugar. Add date mixture. Add flour and mix well. Add nuts and vanilla. Mix again.
3. Pour into greased 9″ x 5″ x 2″ pan. Bake at 325° for 40–45 minutes.

—Eileen Thomas, Millersville, Pennsylvania

Grandma's Crumb Cake

Makes 10–15 servings

> **2 cups brown sugar**
> **1 cup butter or margarine**
> **4 cups flour**
> **2 cups sour milk**
> **2 tsp. baking soda**
> **2 eggs**
> **2 tsp. vanilla**
> **cinnamon**

1. Mix together first 3 ingredients. Reserve 1 cup for topping.
2. Combine sour milk and baking soda. Add eggs and vanilla. Add to flour mixture. Mix by hand just till ingredients are wet.
3. Pour into greased 13" x 8" x 2" pan. Cover with 1 cup topping and sprinkle with cinnamon.
4. Bake at 350° for 40–45 minutes.

I teach in an Amish school and one Friday we made homemade ice cream. On Monday we realized someone had forgotten to take their leftover milk home. I have never seen such sour milk. We decided to save it and make my Grandma's crumb cake! The students were sure anything that bad would kill us. But after the cake was baked even the boys copied down the recipe. It was the best coffee cake I ever made!

—Amy Murray, Orrville, Ohio

Moist Chocolate Cake

Makes 1 long cake

> **2 cups flour, sifted**
> **2 cups sugar**
> **³⁄₄ cup cocoa**
> **2 tsp. baking soda**
> **1 tsp. baking powder**
> **pinch salt**

¹/₂ cup oil
1 cup hot coffee
1 cup milk
2 eggs

1. Mix together flour, sugar, cocoa, baking soda and powder and salt.
2. Make a well in the center of the dry ingredients and add oil, coffee, milk, and eggs. Beat just enough to mix well. (Batter will be lumpy.)
3. Pour into a greased 9″ x 13″ cake pan and bake 35 minutes at 350°.
4. Spread slightly warm cake with Quick Caramel Frosting (or any other favorite!).

Quick Caramel Frosting

¹/₂ cup butter or margarine
1 cup brown sugar
¹/₄ cup milk
1³/₄–2 cups sifted confectioner's sugar

1. Melt butter in saucepan. Add brown sugar and cook over low heat 2 minutes, stirring constantly.
2. Add milk and continue stirring until mixture comes to a boil.
3. Remove from heat and cool. Add confectioner's sugar until frosting reaches spreading consistency.

I confess to being a chocolate freak! This cake is a great pleasure.

—Phyllis Pellman Good, Lancaster, Pennsylvania

Cheesecake Bars

1 cup whole wheat flour
¹/₃ cup brown sugar
6 Tbsp. margarine
8 oz. cream cheese
¹/₄ cup granulated sugar
1 egg
2 Tbsp. milk
2 Tbsp. lemon juice
¹/₂ tsp. vanilla
2 Tbsp. toasted wheat germ
2 Tbsp. walnuts
2 Tbsp. oatmeal

1. Combine flour with brown sugar. Cut in margarine till mixture becomes fine crumbs. Reserve 1 cup and pat remainder in 8" square pan, baking for 15 minutes at 350°.
2. Cream together cheese with sugar. Add egg, milk, lemon juice, and vanilla. Beat well. Spread over crust.
3. Combine 1 cup reserved crumbs with toasted wheat germ, chopped walnuts and oatmeal. Sprinkle over all.
4. Bake at 350° for 20 minutes. Cool and cut in squares.

We enjoy this not-so-sweet bar during the holidays.

—Jessie Hostetler, Portland, Oregon

Springerle

Makes 4 dozen

1 lb. confectioner's sugar
1 lb. flour (4 cups sifted)
1 tsp. baking powder
1 Tbsp. butter, melted
¹/₂ tsp. salt
4 eggs
¹/₄–¹/₂ tsp. anise oil

1. Beat eggs until very thick and lemon colored. Add sugar gradually, then

butter and anise oil. Stir in sifted dry ingredients.
2. Roll out dough to ½" thickness on floured surface with a rolling pin. Using a springerle roller with patterns, roll to approximately ¼" (or less) thickness. Cut with knife and place on greased cookie sheets to dry overnight. Drying is necessary to fix the pattern on the cookie.
3. Bake at 300° for 15–20 minutes until very slightly browned.

These cookies were first served to me when I visited my father's relatives in Alsace (France), and we always have them available at Christmas time.

—Welma Nelson, Elkhart, Indiana

Carob Peanut Bars

Makes 70 1½"-bars

> **3 cups flour**
> **1 cup butter or margarine**
> **1½ cups brown sugar**
> **½ tsp. salt**

1. Cream all ingredients together and press into 10" x 15" cookie sheet.
2. Bake at 375° for 8–10 minutes.

Topping

> **6-oz. pkg. butterscotch chips**
> **1 cup carob chips**
> **½ cup light corn syrup**
> **3 Tbsp. butter**
> **3 Tbsp. water**
> **3 cups peanuts**

1. Melt first 5 ingredients together. Add peanuts.
2. Spread over crust.
3. Bake at 375° for 8–10 minutes. Cool, then cut.
Note: Do not bake longer than time given either first or second time. The bars dry out quickly.

—Mae Imhoff, Roanoke, Illinois

Granola Breakfast Bars

Makes 24 servings

> **2 cups oats**
> **1 cup whole wheat flour**
> **¼ cup soy flour**
> **¼ cup dry milk powder**
> **¼ cup wheat germ**
> **¼ cup rye flour**
> **1 tsp. cinnamon**
> **½ cup honey**
> **½ cup oil**
> **½ cup milk**
> **½ cup coconut, shredded**
> **½ cup sunflower seeds**

1. Mix first 7 ingredients. Add remaining ingredients.
2. Spread ¼″ thick on greased cookie sheets.
3. Bake at 400° for 12–15 minutes. Cut into bars while still warm.

We enjoy these bars at our breakfast table or as part of a car-travel menu.

—Glenda Knepp, Turner, Michigan

Danish Aebleskiver

> **2 cups flour**
> **½ tsp. salt**
> **1½ tsp. baking soda**
> **1½ tsp. baking powder**
> **2 cups buttermilk**
> **3 eggs, separated**
> **1 tsp. vanilla**
> **3 Tbsp. butter, melted**

1. Sift together dry ingredients. Mix all ingredients except the egg whites. Beat whites separately, and fold in last with butter.
2. Fry in oiled aebleskiver pan. When bottom is done, flip aebleskiver with

fork and complete frying.

When our two daughters were quite young we adopted this Danish pancake as our traditional Christmas breakfast. Now our son-in-law enjoys it along with us.

—Wilfred and Erma Martens, Fresno, California

Poertzelki

1¹/₄ cups milk
³/₄ cup sugar (optional)
3 Tbsp. oil
3 eggs, beaten
1 tsp. salt
3¹/₂ cups flour
1 pkg. yeast
¹/₄ cup water
1 Tbsp. sugar
2 cups raisins
sugar

1. Combine first 5 ingredients. Heat to lukewarm. Add 2 cups flour.
2. Dissolve yeast in ¹/₄ cup water and 1 Tbsp. sugar. Add to milk mixture. Mix well. Allow dough to rise till doubled. Add remaining flour and raisins. Let rise till double.
3. Fry walnut-size pieces in hot fat, about 375°, until golden brown, turning once.
4. Roll in sugar while still warm.

Note: I find that omitting the ³/₄ cup sugar helps the poertzelki not to get too brown. Since they are rolled in sugar anyhow, the sugar is not needed in the dough.

We enjoy munching on New Year's cookies while we visit with friends or watch the football games on New Year's Day. They make a nice day-long snack.

—Wilfred and Erma Martens, Fresno, California

Raisin Crisp

Makes 15–18 servings

> *¹/₂ cup sugar*
> *2 Tbsp. cornstarch*
> *1 lb. raisins*
> *1 cup water*
> *2 Tbsp. lemon juice*

1. Mix sugar and cornstarch. Add raisins. Mix well. Add water and cook until slightly thickened.
2. Remove from heat. Add lemon juice. Cool.

Crumbs

> *1³/₄ cups flour*
> *¹/₂ tsp. baking soda*
> *1 cup brown sugar*
> *¹/₄ tsp. salt*
> *1¹/₂ cups quick oatmeal*
> *³/₄ cup butter*
> *cinnamon (optional)*

1. Mix together first 5 ingredients. Cut in butter to make crumbs.
2. Put ¹/₂ of crumbs in bottom of 9″ x 13″ x 2″ pan. Pour raisin mixture over crumbs. Spread out and top with remaining crumbs. Sprinkle with cinnamon.
3. Bake at 400° for 30 minutes.
4. Cool before cutting into squares.

—Alta Ranck, Lancaster, Pennsylvania

Lemon Cookies

Makes 8 dozen cookies

> **1 cup butter or margarine**
> **1¼ cups sugar**
> **1 egg**
> **½ tsp. salt**
> **1 tsp. lemon flavoring**
> **1 Tbsp. baking ammonia**
> **1 cup milk, warmed**
> **3½ cups flour for thin cookies or 4 cups flour for thick drop or
> rolled cookies**

1. Cream butter or margarine. Add sugar and egg, salt and flavoring. Add baking ammonia to warmed milk and add to first mixture alternately with flour. Mix thoroughly.
2. Chill dough for rolled cookies. Bake at 375° for 6–8 minutes according to size of cookies.

Hartshorn, or baking ammonia, has been almost entirely replaced in home use by baking powder. It has many names—baker's ammonia, crystalline ammonia, and ammonium carbonate. It is not for sale at grocery stores, but may be bought at a pharmacy. I understand it is popular with professional pastry chefs whose reputation depends on the long-lasting crispness of their cookies.

Mennonites from Russia used a great deal of baking ammonia in their early years in America, a tradition brought with them from their former homeland where baking powder was unavailable. At Christmastime, my mother always baked many varieties of these cookies—crisp, soft, filled, decorated, plain—because of their long-lasting qualities. Peppermint was a favorite flavor. Recipes were exchanged, sometimes guarded. Some were made without any fat or oil and yet kept well. You will probably notice a sharp odor when you take them from the oven.

—Katie Funk Wiebe, Hillsboro, Kansas

Vanilla Pretzel Cookies

Makes 3 dozen

> **2 cups flour**
> **3/4 cup confectioner's sugar**
> **2 egg whites, unbeaten**
> **2/3 cup butter, softened**
> **1 tsp. vanilla**

1. Mix all ingredients till blended. Shape into ball and wrap in cellophane. Chill.
2. Using a rounded teaspoon of dough, roll into strips. Shape like pretzels on ungreased cookie sheets.
3. Bake at 350° for 10–12 minutes till light golden brown.
4. Cool on rack and spread with or dip into vanilla glaze.

Vanilla Glaze

> **1/2 cup confectioner's sugar**
> **1 Tbsp. butter, melted**
> **1/4 tsp. vanilla**
> **3–4 Tbsp. light cream or milk**

Mix all ingredients in bowl.
Note: I usually double the glaze recipe and dip the cookies. I then place them on a wire rack to dry with waxed paper underneath. It saves clean-up. After they are dried they can be packed to freeze.

— ***Martha Pauls, Regina, Saskatchewan***

Russian Peppernuts

Makes 2 gallons

>   **2 cups dark syrup**
>   **1¹/₂ cups sugar**
>   **¹/₂ cup milk**
>   **³/₄ cup butter or margarine**
>   **coconut milk, from 2 fresh coconuts**
>   **¹/₂ tsp. cloves**
>   **1 tsp. cinnamon**
>   **1 tsp. mace**
>   **¹/₂ tsp. nutmeg**
>   **¹/₂ tsp. allspice**
>   **1 tsp. cardamom**
>   **1 tsp. baking powder**
>   **2 whole fresh coconuts, put through food chopper**
>   **1 tsp. orange extract**
>   **1 tsp. almond extract**
>   **1 tsp. vanilla extract**
>   **1 tsp. maple extract**
>   **9¹/₂ cups flours**
>   **3 orange peels, grated finely**

1. Bring first 5 ingredients to a boil. Boil for 30 seconds. Cool completely.
2. Add remaining ingredients slowly.
3. Knead well till dough is glossy and holds together. Cover and place in cold place for 3–5 days (or even several weeks).
4. Taking small amounts at a time, roll out into thin strips the thickness of a pencil and cut into small pieces. Place pieces on baking sheets.
5. Bake at 350° for 12–15 minutes.

Note: This is a very stiff dough and does not tolerate a very hot oven. Watch carefully while baking.

This is the first time I have ever shared this recipe. It was brought back from Russia by my father, the late Jacob K. Redekopp, and we have treasured it since 1903. These are not soft peppernuts. They were baked before boarding the ship for the long voyage, and were soaked in milk or coffee. They keep for many months in a covered container, and keep tasting better and better with age.

—Mrs. Harvey Harder, Mountain Lake, Minnesota

Peppermint Peppernuts

Makes at least 1 gallon

> **2 cups sugar**
> **1 cup butter or margarine**
> **2 eggs**
> **3 tsp. baking powder**
> **1 tsp. salt**
> **6 cups flour (approximately)**
> **½ cup evaporated condensed milk**
> **¼ cup whole milk**
> **4 tsp. peppermint extract**

1. Cream first 3 ingredients together.
2. Sift together next 3 ingredients.
3. Combine last 3 ingredients and add to creamed mixture, alternately with sifted mixture.
4. Use enough flour to make soft dough. Then refrigerate overnight or longer.
5. Roll out in strips as thick as your finger. Cut the size of hazelnuts, about ³/₄" thick.
6. Bake at 350° for 15 minutes on cookie sheets.

Note: Rolls are easier to handle if frozen in stacked layers with waxed paper between them.

These are for Christmas — before, during and after!

—Elfrieda and Peter Dyck, Akron, Pennsylvania

Oliebollen

Makes 20 oliebollen

> 1 cake brewers yeast (*²/₃ oz.*)
> 1 cup milk
> 2¼ cups flour
> 1 tsp. salt
> 1 egg
> ³/₄ cup raisins, washed
> ³/₄ cup currants
> 1 tart cooking apple, peeled and minced
> fat, for deep frying
> confectioner's sugar, sifted

1. Blend the yeast with ¼ cup lukewarm milk.
2. Sift together flour and salt. Add remaining milk. Mix to a batter with the yeast and egg. Add raisins, currants and apple. Allow to rise till doubled in a warm place.
3. Heat fat to 375°.
4. Shape dough into small balls using 2 metal spoons. Drop into hot fat. Fry about 8 minutes till brown. (Don't fry too slowly.)
5. Place on paper towels to drain.
6. Pile on a dish and cover thickly with confectioner's sugar. Eat while hot.

The process of making and eating oliebollen goes on all New Year's Eve until, or after, midnight. You may have to wish each other Happy New Year with your mouths full!

Traditional New Year's Eve drinks to go with the oliebollen are hot chocolate or hot milk flavored with the seeds of anise.

—Jan Gleysteen, Scottdale, Pennsylvania

Cranberry Christmas Pudding

Makes 12–14 servings

> **2¹/₂ cups flour, sifted**
> **2 tsp. baking powder**
> **¹/₂ tsp. baking soda**
> **1 tsp. salt**
> **³/₄ cup butter or margarine**
> **1¹/₂ cups sugar**
> **2 eggs**
> **1 cup orange juice**
> **1 cup pecans, chopped**
> **1¹/₂ cups cranberries, halved and uncooked**

1. Sift together first 4 ingredients.
2. Cream butter and sugar. Add eggs and beat well. Blend in sifted ingredients alternately with orange juice. Blend in pecans and cranberries with last addition of sifted ingredients.
3. Pour batter into well greased cake pan and bake at 350° for 50–60 minutes.
4. Cool for 5 minutes before cutting. Top with Ruby Red Sauce.

Ruby Red Sauce

> **1¹/₂ cups cranberries**
> **¹/₂ cup water**
> **1 cup sugar**

1. Cook cranberries in water till skins pop. Put through sieve.
2. Add sugar to hot juice and stir till dissolved.

—Luella Gerig, Mishawaka, Indiana
—Barbara Weldy, South Bend, Indiana

Suet Pudding

Makes 6 servings

> *1 cup Karo® syrup or molasses*
> *1 cup sweet milk*
> *1 cup chopped suet or ¹/₂ cup margarine, melted*
> *1 cup raisins*
> *¹/₂ cup currants (optional)*
> *2¹/₂ cups flour*
> *¹/₂ tsp. baking soda*
> *¹/₂ tsp. cinnamon*
> *¹/₂ tsp. nutmeg*
> *¹/₂ tsp. salt*
> *¹/₂ tsp. cloves*

1. Mix all ingredients well.
2. Steam for two hours. Serve warm, with Warm Sauce.

Warm Sauce

> *1 cup brown sugar*
> *4 cups water*
> *5 Tbsp. cornstarch*
> *1 tsp. vanilla*
> *dash of salt*

1. Dissolve the cornstarch in a little of the water.
2. Add remaining ingredients, then cook and stir until thickened. Serve warm.

My one and only "Christmas-food" memory is this Suet Pudding that Mother baked on Christmas Day—with its delicate and spicy aroma and ever-so-mildly flavored sauce.

—Charlotte Croyle, Archbold, Ohio

Snow Pudding

1 Tbsp. gelatin
1/4 cup cold water
1 cup boiling water
1 cup sugar
1/4 cup lemon juice
3 egg whites
dash of salt

1. Soak gelatin in cold water. Dissolve in boiling water. Add sugar and lemon juice. Strain and set aside in refrigerator until the mixture thickens, stirring occasionally. When thick, add stiffly beaten egg whites and continue beating until stiff enough to hold its shape.
2. Mold if desired.

In our family this was always the Christmas dessert served with cookies. Mother tinted half green and half a delicate red. For some of the male members of the family, it was too light, "too much air," but she considered it appropriate after a heavy meal, and the tradition has persisted into the next generations.

—Katie Funk Wiebe, Hillsboro, Kansas

Apricot Sponge

Makes 10–12 servings

1 lb. dried apricots
1 qt. water
hot water
1 pkg. plain gelatin
1/4 cup cold water
1 cup sugar
2 egg whites, stiffly beaten
3–4 tsp. lemon juice, freshly squeezed
whipped cream

1. Cook apricots in 1 quart water till mushy. Drain, reserving juice.
2. Put pulp through vegetable press.

3. Measure out apricot juice and add hot water to make 2 cups.
4. Mix together gelatin and cold water. Add to hot juice, stirring till dissolved.
5. Combine mashed apricots, gelatin and sugar in large mixing bowl. Beat until cold. Fold in egg whites and lemon juice. Pour into mold.
6. Chill and top with whipped cream.

—Elaine Good, Lititz, Pennsylvania

Raspberry Dessert

Makes 14–16 servings

> **1 egg yolk**
> **8 oz. cream cheese**
> **³/4 cup confectioner's sugar**
> **2 tsp. lemon gelatin**
> **1 cup cream, whipped**
> **1 egg white, beaten**
> **1 graham cracker crust**

1. Beat together first 4 ingredients until smooth. Fold in whipped cream and egg white.
2. Pour into crust and chill. Top with topping.

Topping

> **³/4 cup sugar**
> **3 Tbsp. cornstarch**
> **juice from 1 qt. raspberries, frozen and unsweetened**
> **1 qt. raspberries**

1. Heat sugar, cornstarch and juice together till thickened. Add raspberries and cook 5–10 minutes.
2. Cool and top on cheese mixture.

—Verla Fae Haas, Bluesky, Alberta

Date Pudding

Makes 9–10 servings

> 1 cup dates, chopped
> 1 cup water, boiling
> 1 tsp. baking soda
> 1 Tbsp. butter
> 1½ cups flour
> 1 cup sugar
> 1 egg
> ½ cup nuts, chopped
> 1 tsp. vanilla
> ½ cup whipping cream, whipped

1. Combine first 3 ingredients and let cool.
2. Combine next 6 ingredients and mix thoroughly. Add the date mixture. Pour into 8″ x 8″ pan.
3. Bake at 350° for 35 minutes.
4. Break cake into small pieces and fold into whipped cream.

—Fern Hostetler, Altoona, Pennsylvania

Orange Charlotte

Makes 6–8 servings

> 1 Tbsp. gelatin
> 1 cup cold water
> 1 cup boiling water
> 1 cup sugar
> 3 Tbsp. lemon juice
> 1 cup orange juice and pulp
> 3 egg whites, beaten stiffly
> ½ pt. cream
> oranges, peeled and sliced

1. Soak gelatin in cold water.
2. Dissolve in boiling water.

3. Stir sugar, lemon juice, orange juice, pulp and gelatin together.
4. Chill in ice water until thick. When quite thick, beat until frothy. Then add egg whites and fold in whipped cream.
5. Line serving dish with oranges and add mixture. Chill.

—Jean Ann Longacre, Bally, Pennsylvania

Grapenut Pudding

Makes 6–8 servings

> *¹/₂ cup raisins*
> *³/₄ cup grapenuts*
> *1 qt. sweet milk*
> *1 Tbsp. cornstarch*
> *2 eggs, separated*
> *¹/₂ cup sugar*
> *1 tsp. vanilla*

1. Heat raisins and grapenuts in milk, slowly.
2. Mix cornstarch, egg yolks, and sugar. Add to milk.
3. Beat egg whites and add vanilla. Fold into milk mixture.

—Florence Miller, Elizabethtown, Pennsylvania

Brown Rice Pudding

Makes 10–12 servings

>   *¹/₂ lb. brown rice*
>   *water*
>   *1 cup instant dry milk*
>   *2 egg yolks*
>   *¹/₂ cup honey*
>   *¹/₂ cup raisins (optional)*
>   *2 egg whites, stiffly beaten*
>   *cinnamon*

1. Cook rice in water 1″ above layer of dry rice for 30 minutes. Add dry milk.
2. Add small amount of hot rice liquid to egg yolks before adding yolks to mixture on stove. Boil for 1 minute, stirring occasionally.
3. Remove from heat. Add honey and raisins. Cool slightly before adding egg whites.
4. Sprinkle with cinnamon.

—Arlene Mininger, Binghamton, New York

Peanut Brittle

>   *2 cups sugar*
>   *1 cup white corn syrup*
>   *¹/₂ cup water*
>   *1¹/₄ Tbsps. butter*
>   *2 cups raw peanuts*
>   *1 tsp. baking soda*
>   *1 tsp. vanilla*

1. In heavy skillet combine first 3 ingredients. Cook until it threads. Add butter and peanuts. Cook, stirring constantly, till mixture is golden brown.
2. Add baking soda and vanilla. Quickly stir thoroughly. Pour and spread thinly on large greased cookie sheet.
3. Cool quickly in refrigerator or outside if weather is cold.

4. When cold, break into bite-sized pieces.
Note: To test sugar syrup for threading, let syrup drop off spoon above skillet, until it spins a fine thread.

Have a cookie sheet greased before starting recipe.

This is my mother's recipe which we always made once a year just before Christmas. I have continued the tradition with my family. I put it out a little at a time to make it last longer.

It also makes nice gifts at Christmas for friends, neighbors, or the children's school or music teacher.

—Jan Brubacher, Mt. Pleasant, Pennsylvania

Butter Nut Crunch

1 cup sugar
¹/₄ cup water
¹/₂ cup butter (no substitute)
¹/₂ tsp. salt
6-oz. pkg. semi-sweet chocolate chips, melted
1 cup nuts, chopped

1. Combine sugar, water, butter and salt. Heat to boiling. Cook to light crack stage (285°).
2. Grease cookie sheet and pour on mixture. Cool.
3. Spread half of melted chocolate on top of cooked mixture. Sprinkle with ¹/₂ of nuts. Cool quickly.
4. Pour remaining chocolate over and top with remaining nuts. Cool.
5. Break into pieces and serve.

This is our family's favorite Christmas candy.

—Allie Guengerich, Kalona, Iowa

Creamy Caramels

Makes 2 pounds

> **2 cups sugar**
> **1 cup corn syrup**
> **2 cups light cream**
> **¹/₂ tsp. salt**
> **¹/₃ cup butter or margarine**
> **1 tsp. vanilla**
> **¹/₂ cup nuts, optional**

1. Combine sugar, corn syrup, 1 cup cream and salt in heavy saucepan. Cook over medium heat for 10 minutes, stirring constantly during all the cooking. Pour in remaining cream very slowly so mixture does not stop boiling at any time. Cook 5 minutes longer.
2. Stir in butter, 1 Tbsp. at a time. Turn heat low and cook slowly until a small amount of mixture forms a firm ball when dropped in cold water (240°).
3. Remove from heat. Add vanilla and nuts. Mix gently. Cool 10-15 minutes.
4. Stir gently and pour into buttered 8″ x 8″ pan. Cool to room temperature.
5. Cut into ³/₄″ squares and wrap each caramel in waxed paper.

—Hulda Schmidt, Glendive, Montana

Cheese Ball

Makes 20 servings

> 1 lb. cheddar cheese, grated
> 8-oz. pkg. cream cheese
> 2 Tbsp. Worcestershire® sauce
> 1/4 tsp. red pepper
> 2 Tbsp. onion pulp, grated
> 2 oz. dried beef, chopped fine
> 3 oz. pecans, finely chopped

1. Mix all ingredients by hand.
2. Roll in additional pecan pieces and refrigerate.

—Ruth Roth, Rocky Mount, North Carolina

Curried Cheese Ball

Makes 1 cheese ball

> 2 8-oz. pkgs. cream cheese
> 1/2 cup chutney, chopped, or green tomato relish
> 1/2 tsp. dry mustard
> 2 Tbsp. curry powder
> 1/2 cup almonds, toasted and slivered (optional)
> shredded coconut

1. Mix all ingredients thoroughly, except coconut.
2. Shape into balls and roll in coconut.
3. Cover with plastic wrap and chill 1 hour before serving with crackers.

This is a Christmas favorite. We often make cheese balls and give them as Christmas gifts to our cheese-loving friends.

—Joyce Hedrick, Lederach, Pennsylvania

Tomato/Vegetable Juice

Makes 25 quarts

> **1 bushel tomatoes**
> **10 peppers**
> **10 onions**
> **1 bunch parsley**
> **2 cups sugar**
> **$^1/_2$ cup salt**
> **1 tsp. marjoram**
> **1 tsp. thyme**
> **1 tsp. celery salt**
> **1 tsp. pepper**
> **1 tsp. basil**
> **$^1/_4$ tsp. red pepper**

1. Cut up vegetables and cook till soft.
2. Put vegetables through food strainer. Add remaining ingredients.
3. Heat to boiling and can. Process 15 minutes or more.

This is an excellent substitute for orange juice. Peppers are especially rich in vitamin C. This juice is also very useful for tomato soup and any other recipes which call for tomato. We have canned over 100 quarts every year for the past 4 years.

—Kenton Brubaker, Harrisonburg, Virginia

Wassail

Makes 2 quarts

>*6 cups apple cider*
>*3" stick cinnamon*
>*½ tsp. nutmeg*
>*1 Tbsp. whole cloves*
>*1 tsp. lemon rind, grated*
>*3 Tbsp. fresh lemon juice*
>*¼ cup honey*
>*18-oz. can pineapple juice*

Simmer apple cider and cinnamon for 5 minutes, covered. Add remaining ingredients and simmer 5 more minutes.

—Jane Frankenfield, Harleysville, Pennsylvania

Spring

Remembering, then, that in this day of prepared and processed mixes and make-aheads that all of our food comes first from the earth, blest be springtime!

Brilliant in its growth and green, spring brings forth hope, brave tulips, spunky asparagus, stalky rhubarb.

Mix up the Short Cake, there are strawberries coming! We can fix a fresh Korean Spinach Salad. Top it off with Easter Cheese or Hot Cross Buns.

Let the earth bring forth grass, the herb yielding seed, and the fruit tree yielding fruit after his kind, whose seed is in itself, upon the earth.

—Genesis 1:11

Easter Egg Bread

6 individual breads

> *3 cups whole wheat flour*
> *2 Tbsp. active dry yeast*
> *1 tsp. salt*
> *1 cup sugar*
> *1 cup milk*
> *¼ cup butter*
> *¼ cup water*
> *3 eggs, beaten*
> *½ tsp. lemon extract*
> *3–4 cups white flour*
> *6 eggs, hard-cooked, cold, and colored with food coloring*

1. In large bowl combine whole wheat flour, yeast, salt, and sugar.
2. Scald milk and add butter. Stir until butter melts.
3. Add water. Stir into flour mixture.
4. Add eggs and lemon extract.
5. Add part of white flour and beat until smooth.
6. Using the remaining flour, knead dough well, adding flour as needed.
7. Grease bowl, put dough in, turning once to grease surface. Put in warm place to rise until doubled (about 2 hours).
8. Punch down. Divide dough into 6 equal pieces.
9. Take one piece, pinch off about one-fourth of it and set it aside. Shape the larger portion into a flat, round cake, about ½" thick. Place on greased baking sheet.
10. Gently press a hard-cooked egg into center of dough. Shape remaining piece of dough into two rounded strips, 6" long. Lay over egg in an X and tuck ends under loaf.
11. Repeat for the other five pieces and eggs, placing each one on a greased baking sheet, allowing 1" between them.
12. Make 6 collars out of a double thickness of aluminum foil, each one 6" in diameter and ¾" high. Set one around each loaf. Let dough rise until nearly doubled (about 1 hour).
13. Bake at 350° for 20 minutes or until golden.

This is a springtime celebration of Easter!

—Elaine W. Good, Lititz, Pennsylvania

Paska

Makes 6 loaves

> **2 Tbsp. dry yeast**
> **1 cup warm water**
> **1 Tbsp. sugar**
> **12 eggs**
> **2 cups sugar**
> **1 cup orange juice, slightly warmed**
> **1 cup shortening**
> **1 cup oil**
> **1 cup cream (half and half)**
> **2 lemon rinds, finely grated**
> **16 cups flour**

1. Dissolve yeast and 1 Tbsp. sugar in warm water. Set aside.
2. Beat eggs and sugar till light. Add warmed orange juice.
3. Melt shortening. Add oil and cream. Mixture should be lukewarm. Add to egg mixture. Add dissolved yeast. Add lemon rinds. Beat in 8 cups of flour with mixer until bubbly. Gradually knead in remaining 8 cups of flour until dough is smooth. Let rise in warm place until doubled.
4. Shape into balls to fill various-sized tin cans. Tins should be about half full. Allow to rise till dough comes over tops of tins.
5. Bake for 45 minutes at 300°. Remove carefully.

I got this recipe from my mother who is 80 years old now. The lemon rind is unique to this recipe and gives the bread a moisture which is often lacking in other Paskas.

Every Easter I bake this large batch so that each of our five boys gets one (baked in tins in graduated sizes).

As they bake they rise, looking like mushrooms by the time they are done. Then I cover them with icing, each tinted in a different shade, and dot them with sprinkles.

With a touch of Easter grass and a chocolate egg or two, these make lovely plates of goodies for an early morning Easter surprise for the children.

—Alfreda Krahn, Winnipeg, Manitoba

Hot Cross Buns

Makes 4 dozen buns

  2 cups warm water
  1/2 cup sugar
  2 packages dry yeast
  2/3 cup dry milk
  1/2 cup butter, softened
  2 eggs
  2 tsp. salt
  2 cups flour
  1/2 cup candied citron, chopped
  1/2 cup golden raisins
  5–5 1/2 cups flour
  confectioner's sugar

1. Mix first three ingredients in large bowl and dissolve yeast thoroughly.
2. Stir in next seven ingredients by hand or mixer. Stir in remaining flour and knead till smooth and elastic.
3. Let rise in warm place until doubled. Punch down and let rise another 30 minutes.
4. Turn out on floured surface and roll 1/4 to 1/2 inch thick. Cut dough into 2 1/2 inch squares and let rise on greased cookie sheets until doubled.
5. Cut a cross in the top of each bun with a sharp scissors and bake at 400° for 15–20 minutes.
6. Remove from oven and sprinkle crosses with confectioner's sugar.

This makes a tasty Good Friday or Easter morning breakfast.

—Welma Nelson, Elkhart, Indiana

Spring Onion Soup

Makes 6 servings

1/4 cup butter
2/3 cup green onions and tops, thinly sliced
1/2 cup celery, finely diced
1/4 cup flour
1 1/2 tsp. salt
dash pepper
1/2 tsp. Accent®
4 cups milk
1 cup chicken broth
1/2 cup sharp cheese, shredded
toast squares

1. Melt butter in large saucepan. Add onion and celery and cook until tender, but not browned.
2. Blend in flour, salt, pepper, and Accent®. Gradually stir in milk and chicken broth. Cook until thickened, stirring constantly.
3. Stir in cheese.
4. Pour soup into heated bowls and top with toast squares.

—*Mrs. Mark Showalter, Jr., Broadway, Virginia*

Fisherman's Chowder

Makes 6 servings

1/2 cup butter or margarine, melted
1 cup onion, chopped
1 cup celery, sliced
1 1/2 cups carrots, sliced
2 cups cabbage, shredded
2 cups tomato juice
2 7-oz. cans tuna
1 qt. water
1 tsp. salt
1/4 tsp. pepper

1 Tbsp. dry mustard
1 tsp. dill seed
1 cup cultured sour cream

1. Add vegetables to melted butter and sauté until tender, stirring occasionally.
2. Add tomato juice, tuna, water, and seasonings. Cook, covered for 30 minutes, stirring occasionally.
3. Add sour cream and mix well. Heat through, but do not boil.

This chowder tastes particularly good on Spring days when the thermostat is turned down and the fickle weather means that the house becomes almost colder than during the winter.

—Charlotte Croyle, Archbold, Ohio

Spiced Peach Salad

Makes 6 servings

1 can sliced peaches
2 Tbsp. vinegar
2 Tbsp. lemon juice
1/2 cup sugar
1 tsp. whole cloves
1 cinnamon stick or 1/8 tsp. ground cinnamon
3-oz. box orange gelatin
3/4 cup cold water

1. Drain peaches, reserving 3/4 cup syrup. Chop peaches coarsely.
2. Combine vinegar, lemon juice, sugar, and spices. Bring to boil. Add peaches and simmer 10 minutes.
3. Strain to remove cloves and cinnamon stick. Add enough boiling water to make 1 cup.
4. Add gelatin and dissolve. Add cold water and peaches.
5. Cool until slightly thickened. Pour into mold. Chill until firm.

—Marilyn Forbes, Lutherville, Maryland

Creamy Lettuce

Makes 6 servings

> 1½ qts. cutting lettuce (oakleaf or black-seeded simpson are
>   especially good!)
> ½ can evaporated milk (whole milk is better than skim)
> ⅓ cup sugar
> 1 Tbsp. vinegar

1. Fill a 1½ qt. serving dish heaping full of washed, drained lettuce. Set
   aside.
2. Stir together milk and sugar. Add vinegar 1 tsp. at a time until dressing
   is creamy and thick.
3. Pour over lettuce and serve.

This is served as early in spring as I have lettuce growing and ready to use.

—Elaine W. Good, Lititz, Pennsylvania

Springtime Salad

6 servings

> ¼ cup sour cream
> 2 Tbsp. mayonnaise
> 1 Tbsp. vinegar
> 1 tsp. sugar
> ½ tsp. salt
> dash pepper
> ¼ tsp. garlic powder or 1 clove garlic, pressed
> 1 Tbsp. chives, chopped
> 1 Tbsp. parsley, chopped
> dash Tabasco® or cayenne pepper
> 4–5 cups crisped garden lettuce
> 2 cups fresh small spinach leaves
> 3 small green onions, chopped (include tops)
> 6–8 radishes, sliced
> 2 eggs, hard-cooked and sliced

1. Combine all ingredients for dressing, except lettuce, spinach, onions, and radishes.
2. Arrange lettuce, spinach, onions, and radishes in salad bowl. Toss greens with dressing. Garnish with 2 hard-cooked eggs, sliced.

—Doris Longacre

Korean Spinach Salad

Makes 6–8 servings

> 1 lb. fresh spinach
> 1 cup fresh bean sprouts
> 1 small can water chestnuts
> 2 hard-boiled eggs, sliced
> 5 strips bacon, fried and crumbled
> 1 cup mushrooms, sliced (optional)

Toss together lightly.

Dressing

> 1 cup salad oil
> 3/4 cup sugar
> 1/4 cup red garlic wine vinegar
> 1/3 cup catsup
> 1 medium onion, finely chopped
> 2 tsp. Worcestershire® sauce
> salt to taste

Combine ingredients and mix well with salad. Chill before serving.

One of our dinner guests some time ago insisted his wife serve this for his birthday dinner instead of birthday cake!

—Mae Imhoff, Roanoke, Illinois

Fresh Dandelion Salad

1 qt. young dandelion greens
3 eggs, hard boiled (optional)

Cut fine-leafed, young dandelion stalks in early spring. Wash carefully, then chop or tear into 1" inch long pieces.

Cover with dressing and serve.

Dressing 1

2–3 slices bacon
1 egg
3 Tbsp. vinegar
3 Tbsp. water
⅓ cup sugar

Gently fry bacon. Drain and crumble. Beat together egg, vinegar, water, and sugar. Pour into hot bacon drippings. Stir and cook until thickened and bubbly. While still hot pour over dandelion. Garnish with crumbled bacon and sliced hard-boiled eggs.

—Elaine Good, Lititz, Pennsylvania

Dressing 2

½ cup sour cream
1 Tbsp. vinegar
1 tsp. sugar
½ tsp. salt

Mix together sour cream, vinegar, sugar, and salt. Add water to thin, if desired. Pour over greens.

—Elaine Good, Urbana, Illinois

Dressing 3

2–3 slices bacon
3 Tbsp. flour

3 Tbsp. sugar
1 Tbsp. vinegar
dash salt

Brown bacon. Drain and crumble. Stir flour into the drippings. When smooth, add water, a tablespoon at a time, until the liquid reaches a gravy consistency. Add sugar, vinegar, and a dash of salt.

Simmer for 10 minutes and allow to cool. Pour over greens, then garnish with bacon and hard-boiled eggs.

—Edna Brunk, Upper Marlboro, Maryland

Note: These dressings can be used on either fresh endive or spinach also.

We always ate Fresh Dandelion Salad when we first returned in the spring to Ohio after spending the winter in Florida. Dandelion was served with potatoes cooked in their jackets.

—Edna Brunk

When my grandmother came to Illinois as a new bride she brought dandelion seeds to plant in her garden so she'd be sure to have greens for salad!

Today dandelions rank with morning glories, hollyhocks, sunflowers, and multi-flora roses on my farmer-father's list of "plants to keep off the farm!"

—Elaine Good, Urbana, Illinois

Spinach Rice Salad

Makes 10–12 servings

> **2 cups brown rice, cooked and cooled**
> **1 small onion, chopped and browned**
> **1 cup Italian salad dressing**
> **2 Tbsp. soy sauce**
> **1¹/₃ tsp. sugar**
> **¹/₃ lb. fresh spinach, cut into thin strips**
> **¹/₂ cup green onions, sliced**
> **¹/₃ cup bacon, fried and crumbled**

1. Combine salad dressing, soy sauce, and sugar. Stir into cooked rice. Cover and chill.
2. Fold in spinach, onion, and bacon.
3. Let marinate overnight before serving.

—Juliene Wise, West Unity, Ohio

Radish Sandwiches

> **bread**
> **butter**
> **radishes**
> **salt**
> **lettuce**

1. Spread butter on bread.
2. Slice radishes very thin and stack on half a piece of bread. Lightly salt to taste.
3. Add lettuce.
4. Fold over and eat!

Variation:
Substitute green onions or fresh chives for radishes.

Mom, my sister, and one brother devoured these every spring while the rest of us winced! They claimed that the butter counteracted the heat of even the latest radishes.

My mother made these for herself after she returned home from school during springtime afternoons.

—*Elaine Good, Urbana, Illinois*

Broccoli Salad

Makes 8–10 servings

> **2 bunches raw broccoli, cut in small pieces**
> **¹/₂ medium red onion, chopped**
> **1 cup raisins**
> **1 lb. bacon, fried and crumbled**

Toss together lightly.

Dressing

> **1 cup mayonnaise**
> **¹/₄ cup sugar**
> **2 Tbsp. vinegar**

Combine ingredients and mix with broccoli mixture. Marinate 1-3 hours.

—*Elvera Suderman, Newton, Kansas*

Variation:
A handful of roasted peanuts makes a nice addition to this salad.

—*Marilyn Forbes, Lutherville, Maryland*

Creamed Asparagus with Peas

Makes 6 servings

> **2 cups fresh asparagus, broken into small pieces**
> **1 cup fresh or frozen peas**
> **½ cup water**
> **3 Tbsp. flour**
> **⅔ cup milk**

1. Cook vegetables in water until they are nearly tender.
2. Shake flour and milk together in a covered jar.
4. Stir into vegetables and continue stirring until mixture thickens. Add salt and pepper to taste.

I've always loved this dish! It was only when I began cooking for my family while I was in my teens that I discovered the peas were added to stretch whatever asparagus the garden yielded to feed six people!

—Elaine Good, Urbana, Illinois

Sautéed Asparagus with Eggs

> **fresh asparagus**
> **flour**
> **2–3 Tbsp. butter or margarine**
> **3–4 eggs**
> **salt**
> **pepper**

Break fresh asparagus into bite-sized pieces. (By breaking the stalks one can tell which are tender.) Dust each with flour.

Melt butter or margarine. Sauté floured asparagus until it is tender but firm.

Make 3–4 wells in the cooked asparagus and break an egg into each well. Sprinkle asparagus and eggs with salt and pepper. Cover pan and steam until eggs are set.

This is a springtime recipe my mother created because we raised acres of aspar-

agus for market and had lots to eat for ourselves.

—Edna Brunk, Upper Marlboro, Maryland

Asparagus Chinese Style

Makes 6 servings

> **1 Tbsp. peanut or salad oil**
> **¹/₂ cup pork, finely diced**
> **2 cups asparagus, finely sliced on the diagonal**
> **1¹/₂ cups chicken broth, boiling**
> **¹/₂ tsp. salt**
> **1 tsp. Accent®**
> **1 Tbsp. cornstarch**
> **2 Tbsp. water**

1. Heat oil in a skillet. Add pork. Stir for 2 minutes. Add asparagus and stir for 1 minute.
2. Bring chicken broth to a boil, then add it and seasoning to asparagus. Let cook for 3 minutes.
3. Mix cornstarch and water. Add to asparagus and cook until slightly thickened.
4. Serve immediately over cooked rice.

—Phyllis Schmidt, Middlebury, Indiana

Asparagus Ham Bake

Makes 6 servings

1 cup rice, cooked
10½ oz. can of cream of mushroom soup
¾ cup milk
2 cups ham, cooked and cubed
3 Tbsp. chopped onion
1½ cups asparagus, cooked
1 cup bread crumbs, buttered

1. Combine first 5 ingredients. Mix well.
2. Pour half of mixture into a 1½ quart casserole dish. Cover with asparagus. Add remaining half of mixture. Cover with bread crumbs.
3. Bake at 375° for 45 minutes.

—*Mildred Graybill, Freeport, Illinois*

Chicken Yoga

Makes 6 servings

6 pieces of chicken, or whole broiler, cut up
2 cups plain yogurt
½ tsp. basil or thyme, or ¼ tsp. of both

1. Dip each piece of chicken in yogurt and place in greased, 2″ high baking dish. Pour remaining yogurt over the chicken.
2. Sprinkle basil or thyme over the chicken.
3. Cover and bake at 325° for 50 minutes. Remove cover to brown the chicken and bake for an additional 10 minutes.

—*Wanda Pannabecker, Bluffton, Ohio*

Time-Saver Chicken and Rice

Makes 6–8 servings

> **1½ cups uncooked white or brown rice**
> **3 Tbsp. onion, minced**
> **¼ cup celery, chopped**
> **½ cup white flour**
> **¾ tsp. salt**
> **½ cup butter or margarine**
> **3 cups water or chicken broth (or combination)**
> **1¾ cups milk**
> **6–8 servings broiler-fryer chicken**
> **seasoned salt**

1. Grease a 9″ x 13″ pan. Sprinkle in rice.
2. Top with onions and celery.
3. Dust on flour and salt.
4. Dot with butter or margarine.
5. Pour liquids over.
6. Arrange chicken on top and sprinkle with seasoned salt.
7. Cover tightly with aluminum foil and bake at 325° for 2 hours or until chicken is tender.

This is the meal we customarily serve to our children's schoolteachers when we entertain them and their families for an evening each spring.

—Elaine W. Good, Lititz, Pennsylvania

Fresh Catch

Makes 6 servings

3 trout
2–3 Tbsp. oil

1. Remove heads and entrails from fish, but leave skin, tails, and fins intact.
2. Wash fish well and pat dry.
3. Heat oil in frying pan. When hot, lay in fish, being careful of spattering oil.
4. Fry on first side for several minutes until skin is crisp and golden.
5. Turn carefully with tongs and fry on second side until tender. Remove to a warm platter.
6. With tongs grasp the tail and lift. The meat should fall easily away from the bones. Turn bones over and remove meat from the other side.
7. Discard bones, checking meat for fin bones and any others that may have been left behind.
8. Serve immediately with lemon juice, ketchup, or a dash of salt.

First day of trout season comes in mid-April in Pennsylvania. Our avid fisherman-son provides us with as many meals as his time and skill can manage!

—Elaine W. Good, Lititz, Pennsylvania

Tuna Casserole

Makes 6 servings

> 3 cups noodles, uncooked
> 3 Tbsp. butter or margarine
> 3 Tbsp. flour
> ¹/₂ tsp. salt
> pepper to taste
> 1¹/₂ cups milk
> ³/₄ cup cheese, cubed
> 7-oz. can tuna, drained
> 2 slices bread, cubed
> 4 Tbsp. butter or margarine, melted

1. Cook noodles in salted water. Drain.
2. Melt 3 Tbsp. butter. Add flour and salt and stir until smooth. Add milk and cheese and stir until smooth.
3. Place half of the cooked noodles in a greased casserole. Pour half of the cheese sauce over the noodles.
4. Spread tuna over sauce, followed by the remaining noodles, and then the remaining sauce.
5. Toss bread crumbs in butter, then sprinkle over top.
6. Bake covered at 350° for 45–60 minutes. Uncover at end of baking time, long enough to brown bread cubes.

Eating this tuna casserole always brings back a picture of Mother's good china and a crisp white tablecloth. We were poor, but I was never aware of that poverty, partly because our mother knew how to create beauty out of little.

Her Tuna Casserole had a place of honor in Mother's one silver, covered casserole dish. Unfortunately, I never found her recipe, so I've experimented until I came up with the taste I remember.

—Charlotte Croyle, Archbold, Ohio

Short Cake

Makes 1 square cake

1 egg
½ cup milk
2 Tbsp. butter
½ cup sugar
2 cups flour
½ tsp. salt
2 tsp. baking powder

1. Beat the egg, then add all other ingredients and mix well together.
2. Grease a square baking dish and bake at 350° for 30 minutes or until a toothpick comes out clean.
3. Cut into squares and serve with fresh strawberries.

I have tried other short cake recipes and always conclude that my Grandma Kraybill's is the best.

—Jean Kraybill Shenk, Mount Joy, Pennsylvania

Rhubarb Cake

Makes 1 long cake

1¹/₂ cups brown sugar or granulated sugar
¹/₂ cup butter
1 egg
1 tsp. vanilla
1 tsp. baking soda
¹/₂ tsp. salt
2 cups flour
1 cup sour milk or buttermilk
1¹/₂ cups rhubarb, finely chopped
¹/₂ cup sugar
1 tsp. cinnamon

1. Cream sugar and butter. Add egg and vanilla. Beat.
2. Sift baking soda, salt, and flour. Add alternately with sour milk to creamed mixture. Add rhubarb and mix well. Pour batter into 9″ x 12″ pan.
3. Mix sugar and cinnamon together and sprinkle over top. Bake at 350° for 35–40 minutes.

—Anne Loewen, Altona, Manitoba
—DeElda Hershberger, Milford, Nebraska
—Helen Miller, Lancaster, Pennsylvania

Warm Sauce

1 cup brown sugar
1 cup granulated sugar
1 cup light cream
2 tsp. flour
2 tsp. vanilla
¹/₂ cup butter

Combine in saucepan and cook till smooth and creamy.
Note: I also freeze rhubarb and make this dessert in late winter as a refreshing taste. It's something new to make after the winter blahs.

—DeElda Hershberger, Milford, Nebraska

Rosy Red Rhubarb Cake

Makes 1 long cake

Crust

> **2 cups flour, sifted**
> **2¹/₂ tsp. baking powder**
> **¹/₄ tsp. salt**
> **¹/₄ cup brown sugar**
> **¹/₂ cup shortening**
> **1 egg**
> **³/₄ cup milk**

1. Mix together first four ingredients. Cut shortening into mixture. Beat egg. Add it and milk.
2. Spread crust on bottom and sides of ungreased 9″ x 13″ pan.

Filling

> **6 cups rhubarb, finely sliced**
> **3-oz. package strawberry gelatin**

Fill crust with rhubarb and sprinkle with gelatin.

Topping

> **1¹/₂ cups sugar**
> **¹/₂ cup flour**
> **6 Tbsp. butter, softened**

1. Blend ingredients. Sprinkle over rhubarb and gelatin.
2. Bake at 350° for 50 minutes.

Note: Other fruit can be substituted for the rhubarb, such as fresh peaches with orange gelatin or blueberries with lemon gelatin. With other fruits, the sugar may be reduced.

—Rita Yoder, Irwin, Pennsylvania

Rhubarb Torte

Makes 1 square cake

Crust

>1 cup flour
>pinch of salt
>2 Tbsp. sugar
>1/2 cup butter

1. Mix flour, salt, and sugar together. Cut in butter until particles the size of peas are formed.
2. Press into 8″ x 8″ or 9″ x 9″ baking pan. Bake at 350° for 20–25 minutes.

Filling

>1 1/2 cups sugar
>2 Tbsp. flour
>1/3 cup milk
>3 egg yolks
>3 cups rhubarb, cut up

1. While crust is baking mix filling ingredients and cook until rhubarb is tender.
2. Pour into crust. Top with meringue and brown under the broiler.

Meringue

>3 egg whites, stiffly beaten
>1/4 tsp. cream of tartar
>6 Tbsp. sugar

Combine and mix well.

This recipe is originally from Muriel Neve, a missionary in Hokkaido who has moved elsewhere in Japan and left me the mantle of preparing this absolutely delicious rhubarb dessert. In northern Japan the rhubarb season runs into July.

—Mary Beyler, Kushiro, Japan

Rhubarb Pie

Makes 9" pie

> 1¹/₂ *cups sugar*
> ¹/₄ *tsp. salt*
> 3 *Tbsp. quick tapioca*
> 1 *tsp. orange rind, grated*
> 2 *Tbsp. butter*
> 6 *cups rhubarb, diced*
> 9" *pie shell, unbaked*
> 1 *pie lattice*

1. Mix all ingredients (except pie shell) and cook for 3 minutes in heavy saucepan.
2. Pour mixture into pie shell and place lattice on top. Bake at 425° for 35–40 minutes.

I often took this to the end-of-school picnic when our children were young.

—Esther B. Heatwole, Rocky Ford, Colorado

Rhubarb Pie

Makes 9" pie

> 5–6 *cups rhubarb, cut up*
> 3-oz. *package raspberry or strawberry gelatin*
> 1 *egg, slightly beaten*
> 2¹/₄ *Tbsp. minute tapioca*
> ¹/₂ *cup sugar*
> 1 *unbaked 9" pie shell*
> 1 *unbaked lattice pie top*

1. Mix all filling ingredients together. Pour into pie shell.
2. Cover filling with lattice pie top, or pie crust with plenty of air holes.
3. Bake at 425° for 35–40 minutes.

I usually use the first spring rhubarb to make five pies for the staff where my husband teaches school. This is a once-a-year happening. The teachers call it a sign of spring. It helps to make their day and mine also.

—Florence Voegtlin, Tofield, Alberta

Rhubarb Pie

Makes 9" pie

> **1¹/₂ cups cold water**
> **1 cup sugar**
> **4 Tbsp. cornstarch**
> **¹/₄ cup sugar**
> **1¹/₂ cups rhubarb, diced**
> **3 egg yolks**
> **9" pie shell, baked**

1. Mix water and 1 cup sugar in saucepan. Heat. Add cornstarch and ¹/₄ cup sugar. Cook till thick. Add rhubarb and cook till tender.
2. Add small amount of rhubarb sauce to egg yolks. Beat well. Add remaining rhubarb sauce. Let cool slightly, then pour into pie shell.
3. Cover top with meringue and bake at 350° for 12 minutes.

Meringue

> **3 egg whites**
> **¹/₄ tsp. cream of tartar**
> **6 Tbsp. sugar**
> **¹/₂ tsp. flavoring, if desired**

Beat egg whites and cream of tartar. Gradually add sugar and flavoring.

—Alma K. Bloss, Jackson, Ohio

Lemon Meringue Pie

Makes 1 pie

> **1¹/₂ Tbsp. butter**
> **8 Tbsp. flour**
> **1 cup sugar**
> **¹/₄ tsp. salt**
> **2 egg yolks**
> **2 cups milk**
> **juice of 1 lemon**
> **¹/₂ rind of lemon, grated**
> **1 pie shell, baked**

1. Melt butter.
2. Mix flour, sugar, and salt. Add butter to dry mixture.
3. Beat egg yolks and add milk. Gradually add flour mixture.
4. Cook in heavy kettle or over hot water, stirring constantly until quite thick. Remove from heat. Add lemon juice and rind. Mix well.
5. Pour into baked pie shell. Cover top with meringue and bake at 325° until a delicate brown, about 15 minutes.

Note: Be sure to wait to add lemon juice until mixture has thickened and cooked, otherwise you will have a curdled mess.

Meringue

> **2 Tbsp. confectioner's sugar**
> **2 egg whites, stiffly beaten**

Beat sugar into stiffly beaten egg whites.

—*Miriam E. Shenk, Lancaster, Pennsylvania*

Creamy Strawberry Pie

Serves 6 or 7

> **9″ graham cracker pie shell**
> **1 quart fresh strawberries or other fruit**
> **1 cup water**

1 package unflavored gelatin
1¼ cups cottage cheese
¼ cup sugar
3 Tbsp. sugar
1 Tbsp. cornstarch

1. Combine in saucepan ½ cup water and unflavored gelatin. Stir gelatin mixture over low heat until gelatin dissolves. Cool to room temperature.
2. Combine in blender 1 cup strawberries, cottage cheese, ¼ cup sugar, and cooled gelatin mixture. Whirl a few minutes until smooth and creamy.
3. Pour into pie shell. Chill 1–2 hours or until set.
4. Combine in blender ½ cup water, 1 cup strawberries, 3 Tbsp. sugar, and cornstarch. Whirl until smooth. Transfer mixture to saucepan and cook over low heat, stirring frequently until mixture boils.
5. Cook 2–3 minutes. Cool to room temperature. Pile remaining berries (slice if they are large) onto chilled cottage cheese mixture in the pie shell. Pour cooled glaze over all and chill several more hours.

—Doris Longacre

Fresh Strawberry Pie or Tarts

Makes 9–12 servings

1 qt. strawberries, washed and hulled
¾ cup sugar (more or less if desired)
3-oz. pkg. strawberry gelatin
1 cup hot water
1 cup whipped cream
2 8″ pie shells, baked, or 9 3½″ tart shells, baked

1. Combine strawberries and sugar. Let stand 10 minutes.
2. Dissolve gelatin in water. Pour over berries. Chill until gelatin begins to thicken.
3. Fold 4 Tbsp. gelatin into whipped cream and chill 5–10 minutes.
4. Place a layer of whipped cream into bottom of each pie shell, or tart shell, and chill 10 minutes. Cover with a layer of jelled strawberries, pressing hull end of each berry lightly into cream. Add remaining thickened gelatin to fill the shells. Chill several hours before serving.

—Lillie Cullar, North Lima, Ohio

Strawberry Rhubarb Compote

Makes 6–8 servings

1/2 cup orange juice
3/4 cup sugar
2 lbs. rhubarb, diced
1 pt. fresh strawberries

1. Heat orange juice and sugar till dissolved.
2. Simmer rhubarb 5 minutes. Cool slightly. Add to juice. Add strawberries. Chill.

—Madeline Roth, London, Ontario

Maple Syrup Tarts

Make about 18 tarts

Pastry

2 cups flour
1/2 tsp. salt
1/2 cup confectioner's sugar, sifted
1 tsp. baking powder
3/4 cup shortening
1 egg, mixed with 2 Tbsp. milk

1. Mix flour, salt, sugar, and baking powder together. Cut in shortening with knives or a pastry blender until the particles are the size of peas.
2. Sprinkle with egg and milk, mixing with a fork until the flour is moistened.
3. Gather dough together into a ball. Roll out and cut into pieces to line tart pans.

Filling

2 eggs
1/4 tsp. salt

2 tsp. vinegar
1/2 cup maple syrup
6 Tbsp. butter, melted
2/3 cup nutmeats, chopped

Mix in order and fill tart tins. Bake at 350° for 20 minutes.

—Mrs. K. Alvin Schwartz, Kitchener, Ontario

Rhubarb Dessert

Makes 12–15 servings

6 cups rhubarb, chopped
2 eggs, beaten
1 1/2 cups sugar (according to taste)
4 Tbsp. flour
1 1/3 cups whole wheat flour
1 cup brown sugar (according to taste)
1/2 cup butter or margarine

1. Mix rhubarb and eggs. Sprinkle sugar and flour over mixture and stir in.
2. Pour into greased 9″ x 13″ pan.
3. In same bowl combine remaining ingredients, cutting butter or margarine into flour and sugar until fine crumbs form. Sprinkle over rhubarb.
4. Bake at 350° for 45 minutes.
5. Serve hot with milk. Leftovers may be eaten cold for breakfast!

We eat a lot of this in the spring when fresh rhubarb is available. But it is also good in other seasons if some rhubarb has been preserved in the freezer. You can mix it up without allowing the rhubarb to thaw, but then allow about 10 minutes extra baking time.

—Elaine W. Good, Lititz, Pennsylvania

Rhubarb Ice Cream

Makes about 6 quarts

> **6 cups rhubarb, diced**
> **2 cups sugar**
> **6 eggs**
> **3 cups cream**
> **3/4 cup sugar**
> **3 Tbsp. lemon juice**
> **dash salt**

1. In a heavy saucepan combine rhubarb and 2 cups sugar. Cook over medium heat until bubbly. Reduce heat and cook about 15 minutes until mixture thickens and rhubarb is tender. Set aside to cool.
2. Beat together remaining ingredients. Pour into 6-qt. ice cream freezer can.
3. Add cooled rhubarb and additional cream until the can is as full as you like it.
4. Turn to freeze. Serve immediately!

Note: This can also be made in pans in your freezer. Make as above, except pour into a 9″ x 13″ pan and freeze until soft-firm.

Turn into mixing bowl and beat until smooth. Return to freezer and freeze firm. For this method I suggest that the recipe be reduced by at least one-third.

After the corn is planted on our farm, or if rain comes and interrupts the field work, we take time to make ice cream. In the spring, this is our choice flavor!

—Elaine W. Good, Lititz, Pennsylvania

Strawberry Parfait

Makes 10 servings

> **3 cups fresh strawberries, sliced**
> **2 cups sugar**
> **3 eggs, separated**

8 tsp. sugar
2 cups heavy cream

1. Boil strawberries and sugar. Keeping covered, cook 5 minutes over low heat.
2. Puree mixture in blender. Let cool.
3. In large bowl beat egg yolks with 4 tsp. sugar until mixture ribbons. Add cream. Beat until mixture holds firm peaks.
4. Fold 2½ cups puree into egg and cream mixture.
5. Beat egg whites until stiff. Beat in 4 tsp. sugar and remaining puree. Fold egg white mixture into egg yolk mixture. Pour into 10 1-cup bowls or into a 2½ quart bowl.
6. Freeze at least 6 hours. Remove from freezer 10-20 minutes before serving.

Note: Other berries or peaches can be used instead of strawberries.

— *Ginny Birky, Cortez, Colorado*

Easter Eggs

3 1-lb. boxes confectioner's sugar
⅓ cup mashed potatoes, hot
¾ lb. butter, softened
1 cup coconut
½ cup nuts, chopped
⅓ tsp. vanilla
1 lb. sweet chocolate

1. Combine first six ingredients by hand or spoon. Shape into eggs or smaller balls. Set aside for several days to ripen.
2. Melt chocolate and dip eggs until completely coated. Let dry. Store in cool place.

Note: Age improves flavor.

— *Janet Yoder, Phoenix, Arizona*

Easter Cheese

4 cups fresh unpasteurized milk
4 eggs
2 cups buttermilk
1 tsp. salt
1 tsp. sugar

1. Scald milk but do not boil.
2. Beat eggs till almost frothy. Add buttermilk, salt, and sugar. Beat again. Pour mixture into hot milk.
3. Continue to heat over low heat, stirring gently to keep it from setting, until curds separate from whey. Cover and let stand 10 minutes.
4. Pour through a cheesecloth-lined colander. Gather up edges of cloth so curds form a ball and suspend to drain off all whey.
5. When thoroughly drained, put in a bowl and refrigerate. Serve with maple syrup.

Note: Deciding when the cooking is complete takes experience and depends on the texture you prefer in the finished product. Shorter cooking results in a softer cheese, while too long gives quite a firm, dense product. The cheese is very rich, more like cream cheese than cottage cheese, but not as smooth and fine textured, and slightly yellow. It is served as dessert.

This was a traditional dish served at my home on Easter Sunday—rarely any other time. The eggs may have been an Easter symbol, or perhaps it had more to do with the fact that fresh Ontario maple syrup was available about then. Since my parents are living in a retirement home and no longer cook, one or more of the family usually makes sure they get a taste of Easter cheese—even though the maple syrup is a deviation from a diabetic diet!

—Ferne Burkhardt, Petersburg, Ontario

Rhubarb Punch

Makes 4 quarts

18 cups rhubarb, cut-up
12 cups sugar
1–1½ cups sugar
1 liter ginger ale

1. Simmer rhubarb and water.
2. Strain through fine sieve and add sugar.
3. Chill and add ginger ale. 1 can of pineapple juice may be substituted for
   ½ liter of ginger ale.

Note: Rhubarb juice alone may be canned, then mixed and served at a later
time.

—Anna Mary Brubacher, Kitchener, Ontario

Summer

Summer kitchens steam. Sidewalks bake. The ground cracks and waits for water, drinks and sends up heavy plenty.

We harvest, we preserve, we picnic. We, and the earth, grow intemperate. There are too many peaches, too many beans, we sigh: too few cool hours in these too full days.

But blooming markets and gardens bring us fullness of spirit and health.

Bring on the Gazpacho. Spend only a few minutes at the stove with Beef Teriyaki Stir-Fry. How about watermelon and Rollkuchen?

The earth is full of the goodness of the Lord.

—Psalm 33:5

Crullers

Makes 10–12 servings

> **8 oz. sour cream, cultured**
> **4 eggs**
> **1¹/₂ tsp. salt**
> **4 cups flour**

1. Mix sour cream, eggs, and salt. Add 2 cups of flour and beat. Mix in 1¹/₂ cups flour by hand. Knead remaining flour into dough on floured surface.
2. Divide dough into 4 quarters. Roll out each quarter into a 12″ to 14″ circle. Cut into strips 2″ x 4″. Then cut a slit in each cruller.
3. Bake in deep, hot fat (360°-370°) until golden brown on each side, turning once. (Submerge each cruller completely for a few seconds when first placing it in fat.)
4. Drain on paper towels.

Note: A fluted cutting wheel makes cutting the crullers and slits easier and faster.

Some like crullers crisp, some like them soft. Rolling dough thinner will produce crisper crullers.

We usually have these at summer picnics; 4th of July is a natural. I always serve watermelon with them at these picnics. The next day, if there are any left, they are good with jelly or rhubarb sauce. They may be frozen, but they will crush easily, like potato chips.

—Mildred Stucky, North Newton, Kansas

Rollkuchen

Makes 4 servings

> **2 heaping cups flour, pre-sifted**
> **1 tsp. baking powder**
> **¹/₂ tsp. baking soda**
> **1¹/₄ tsp. salt**
> **2 Tbsp. oil**
> **²/₃ cup milk**
> **1 tsp. vinegar**
> **2 eggs**

1. Mix all ingredients to a soft dough. Allow to set at least ¹/₂ hour.
2. Roll thin and cut into strips.
3. Fry in hot fat, turning only once.

The custom is to serve watermelon and Rollkuchen as the entire meal. It's very refreshing for hot summer days.

—Jean Friesen, Abbotsford, British Columbia

Onion Cheese Bread

Makes 6–8 servings

> **¹/₂ cup onion, chopped**
> **1 Tbsp. shortening**
> **1 cup cheese, grated**
> **1 cup biscuit mix**
> **1 egg, beaten**
> **¹/₃ cup milk**
> **1 Tbsp. poppy or sesame seeds**
> **2 Tbsp. butter, melted**

1. Sauté onions in shortening until light brown. Add onion and ¹/₂ cup cheese to biscuit mix.
2. Combine egg and milk, then add to mixture until mix is moistened.
3. Spread dough in 8″ x 8″ x 1¹/₂″ baking dish. Sprinkle top with remaining

cheese and seeds. Pour on melted butter.
4. Bake at 400° for 20-30 minutes.

This is a quick bread that goes well with summer barbecues.

—Kathy Stoltzfus, Leola, Pennsylvania

Zucchini Bread

Sweet

Makes 1 loaf

> **3 cups flour**
> **1½ cups sugar**
> **1 tsp. cinnamon**
> **1 tsp. salt**
> **1 tsp. baking powder**
> **1 tsp. baking soda**
> **2 cups zucchini, unpeeled and shredded**
> **1 cup nuts, chopped**
> **1 cup raisins**
> **3 eggs**
> **1 cup oil**

1. In large bowl combine first 9 ingredients.
2. Beat eggs and oil together. Pour over flour mixture, and stir till moistened.
3. Bake at 350° for 1½ hours or till toothpick inserted comes out clean, in 9″ x 5″ x 3″ loaf pan.
4. Cool in pan 10 minutes. Turn topside up on rack to cool completely.

—Mrs. Abram Groff, Strasburg, Pennsylvania

Cardamom Braid

Makes 1 braided loaf

1 pkg. yeast
¾ cup warm water
¼ cup sugar
¼ cup butter, softened
½ tsp. salt
¾ tsp. cardamom, ground
1 egg
1 cup whole wheat flour
1¾ - 2 cups white flour
milk
sugar

1. Dissolve yeast in warm water. Add next 6 ingredients. Beat well. Stir in white flour.
2. Knead on floured surface till smooth. Allow dough to rise in greased bowl till double.
3. Divide in thirds. Form into balls. Cover and let rest 10 minutes.
4. Make three 16″ ropes and braid loosely. Place on greased cookie sheet. Cover and let rise till double.
5. Brush with milk and sprinkle lightly with sugar.
6. Bake at 350° for 20-25 minutes.

Note: I usually double this recipe so there is some to freeze for a later date.

Cardamom braid and taco salad are a favorite and frequent summer Sunday dinner in our home. Before leaving for church I'll pull a loaf of cardamom braid out of the freezer, stick it in a paper bag and put it in the back of our car. When church is over we have bread that smells and tastes like it just came out of the oven.

—Sarah Ellen Myers, Jackson, Mississippi

100% Whole Wheat Bread

Makes 4 loaves

> **2 cups water, boiling**
> **¹/₂ cup dry milk, powdered**
> **¹/₂ cup butter**
> **1 tsp. salt**
> **¹/₂ cup honey, or cane molasses**
> **2 Tbsp. yeast**
> **1 cup whole wheat flour**
> **2 eggs, beaten**
> **7 cups whole wheat flour, warmed in oven for few minutes**

1. In a large bowl pour boiling water over dry milk, butter, salt and honey. Allow to cool to 115°-120° (use candy thermometer).
2. Mix dry yeast with 1 cup flour and beaten eggs. Add to milk mixture and beat with electric mixer. Add 2 more cups of flour. Beat 5 minutes. Stir in another 3 cups of flour, using wooden spoon.
3. Turn dough onto floured board and knead, using flour sparingly until smooth and elastic, at least 5 minutes. Cover and let rest for 20 minutes.
4. Punch dough down by kneading a few strokes. Divide into 4 parts, rolling out each with rolling pin. Roll up jelly roll fashion to shape loaves. (Cinnamon bread can be made by spreading with butter, and sprinkling with sugar and cinnamon mixture, then rolled up.) Let rise until doubled and bake, or shape and cover with plastic wrap and refrigerate for 2-24 hours. Remove from refrigerator 10 minutes before baking.
5. Bake at 350° for 30-35 minutes, or until done.

For Cinnamon Rolls

1. Divide raised dough into 3 or 4 parts and roll into rectangular shapes. Spread with butter, and sprinkle with brown sugar and cinnamon mixture. Roll up from long side.
2. Cut into 1″ slices and place cut side up in greased round or rectangular pans. Let rise until doubled, or shape and cover with plastic wrap and refrigerate for 2-24 hours. Remove from refrigerator 10 minutes before baking.
3. Bake at 350° for 25 minutes.

—*Leora Gerber, Dalton, Ohio*

Gazpacho

2 cups tomato juice
1 cup beef broth or consommé
1 cup water
pinch salt
1 tsp. sugar
1 tomato, chopped
1/2 cup carrots, finely chopped
1 Tbsp. onion, chopped
1 cup green peppers, chopped
1 cup cucumbers, chopped
1 cup summer squash, chopped

1. Mix first 4 ingredients in blender, or beat with wire wisk. Stir in next 4 ingredients. Refrigerate several hours, or overnight.
2. At mealtime place remaining chopped vegetables in individual bowls and allow each person to add to the soup what each prefers.

Summer soups are light, cool, economical, and quick. Served with crackers and sliced cheese this makes a refreshing lunch or evening meal.

—**Kathryn Sherer, Goshen, Indiana**

Vegetable Soup

3 qts. tomatoes
2 qts. carrots
2 green peppers
5 medium onions
2 medium heads of cabbage
2 Tbsp. butter
water to desired amount
1/3 cup salt

1. Prepare all vegetables for soup by peeling, dicing, or slicing.
2. Melt butter in large kettle. Add chopped onions and green peppers and cook for 3-5 minutes. Add water and carrots. Cook until carrots are almost done. Add cabbage and continue to cook 5 more minutes before

adding tomatoes. Cook 5-10 more minutes.

Note: This is a very large recipe and can be put in jars and canned. For a family meal the recipe could be cut in half or even by three-fourths.

—Joann Ewert, Modesto, California

Summer Borscht

2 ham hocks, smoked
3-4 cups ham broth
2 qts. beet tops, swiss chard, or spinach, cut-up
1 qt. sour dock (züraump), or 5" stalk of rhubarb, cut-up
1½ cups onion tops, cut-up
2 Tbsp. dill leaves
½ cup sour cream

1. Cook ham hocks till done.
2. Using 3-4 cups of ham broth, add beets, sour dock, onions, and dill leaves. Cook till greens are tender. Add cooked ham.
3. Add sour cream just before serving, and serve over mashed potatoes in soup plates.

—Katie Schultz, Sidney, Montana

Gooseberry Salad

Makes 8 servings

> **2 3-oz. pkgs. lemon gelatin**
> **¹/₂ cup sugar**
> **1¹/₂ cups boiling water**
> **1 small can frozen orange juice**
> **2¹/₂ cups gooseberries (cooked until soft in small amount of water)**
> **2 cups celery, chopped**
> **1 cup nuts, chopped**

1. Combine gelatin, sugar, and water. Stir until dissolved.
2. Add orange juice and gooseberries. Chill until partially set.
3. Stir in celery and nuts. Pour into mold and chill until set.

Note: Gooseberries should be cooked until they split open and are very mushy.

—Jan Buerge, Kansas City, Kansas

Rice Salad

Makes 6 servings

> **2 cups cold, cooked rice**
> **1 apple, diced**
> **1 cup pineapple tidbits**
> **¹/₄ cup red and green peppers, finely diced**
> **1 cup salad dressing**

Combine all ingredients. Mix well. Chill. Garnish with parsley, lettuce, or lemon.

—Madeline Roth, London, Ontario

Molded Fruit Salad

Makes 8 servings

1³/₄ cups fresh or canned pineapple chunks (reserve juice)
3-oz. pkg. lime gelatin
1 cup evaporated milk, chilled
¹/₂ cup nuts, chopped
2 Tbsp. lemon juice
¹/₃ cup mayonnaise
1 cup seedless grapes, halved, or 1 cup mandarin or fresh oranges
    shredded cheddar cheese (optional)

1. Heat to boiling 1 cup juice drained from pineapple chunks. Pour over gelatin and stir until gelatin is dissolved. Chill until thick and syrupy.
2. Whip evaporated milk until stiff.
3. Combine gelatin with other remaining ingredients except cheese. Fold into whipped milk. Pour into mold and chill until set. Before serving, top with shredded cheese.

Note: This recipe can also be used as a second layer of a molded salad. Make first layer of one package of lemon gelatin with one cup shredded cabbage.

—Elva May Roth, Morton, Illinois

Special Vegetarian Salad

Makes 4 servings

> 2 bananas
> 1 Tbsp. lime or lemon juice
> ½ cup golden raisins
> ½ cup salted peanuts
> 1 Tbsp. freshly chopped or dried chives
> 2 cups cooked rice
> ½ cup mayonnaise
> 1 Tbsp. honey
> ½ tsp. curry powder
> dash of Tabasco® sauce

1. Slice bananas. Sprinkle with juice. Gently mix in raisins, peanuts, chives, and rice.
2. Combine remaining ingredients and mix well. Pour over banana mixture and stir gently until well mixed. Chill. Can be served in the center of a honeydew melon or on a bed of lettuce.

—Margret Jutzi, Millbank, Ontario

Six Bean Salad

Makes 12 servings

> 1 can kidney beans
> 1 can lima beans
> 1 can wax beans
> 1 can french-cut green beans
> 1 can straight-cut green beans
> 1 can garbanzo beans (chick peas)
> 1 green pepper, chopped
> 1 large Spanish onion, thinly sliced
> ½ cup red wine vinegar
> ½ cup sugar
> ½ cup salad oil
> 1 tsp. salt

½ tsp. dry mustard
2 Tbsp. dry parsley

1. Combine all beans, pepper, and onion.
2. Combine vinegar, sugar, oil, salt, mustard, and parsley. Pour over beans. Mix well.

A delicious addition to a barbecue meal, Sunday School picnic, baseball barbecue, or family gathering.

—Helen Rose Pauls, Langley, British Columbia

Cauliflower Salad

Makes 6–8 servings

1 head lettuce, finely cut
1 head cauliflower, cut into small pieces
1 small onion, chopped finely
1 lb. bacon, fried crisp, drained, and crumbled
grated parmesan cheese
2 cups (scant) salad dressing
⅓ cup sugar

1. Layer lettuce, cauliflower, onion, and bacon in a dish.
2. Combine salad dressing and sugar. Mix well. Pour over layered vegetables. Cover with grated cheese. Refrigerate. Toss well before serving.
Note: This salad can be made a day in advance, but do not toss until serving time.

—Alta Ranck, Lancaster, Pennsylvania

Cauliflower Bacon Salad

Makes 6–8 servings

> **1 lb. bacon, fried and crumbled**
> **1 large head cauliflower, cut up**
> **6-oz. pkg. bleu cheese, crumbled**
> **8 oz. salad dressing**
> **lettuce greens**

1. Toss together bacon, cauliflower, and cheese. Mix with favorite dressing the night before serving.
2. Serve on lettuce greens.

—Janet Swartzentruber, Worthington, Ohio

Romaine Lettuce Salad

Makes 6–8 servings

> **1 large bunch Romaine lettuce**
> **2 hard-boiled eggs, chopped**
> **6 slices bacon, fried crisp and crumbled**
> **¼ cup onion, chopped or 2 small green onions, chopped**

Tear lettuce. Add all other ingredients and toss. Just before serving, add the following dressing.

Dressing

> **¼ cup salad oil**
> **¼ cup sugar**
> **¼ cup vinegar**
> **⅓ cup ketchup**
> **1 Tbsp. Worcestershire® sauce**
> **½ tsp. salt**

Combine all ingredients. Mix well. Pour over salad.

—Helen White, Edmonton, Alberta

Tomato and Onion Salad

Makes 6–8 servings

> *1 tsp. salt*
> *1 or 2 cloves garlic, minced*
> *1 tsp. sugar*
> *¼ tsp. pepper*
> *2 tsp. prepared mustard*
> *¼ cup salad oil*
> *2 Tbsp. vinegar*
> *6 firm tomatoes, sliced*
> *1 onion, thinly sliced*
> *parsley, chopped*

1. Combine salt and garlic. Mash with spoon. Stir in sugar, pepper, mustard, oil, and vinegar. Beat together well.
2. Pour over tomato and onion slices, and sprinkle with parsley. Chill.
3. Serve without dressing.

—Miriam E. Shenk, Lancaster, Pennsylvania

Sweet-Sour Tomatoes

> *4 medium to large ripe tomatoes*
> *½ cup olive oil or good vegetable oil*
> *½ cup red wine vinegar*
> *2 Tbsp.–¼ cup sugar (according to taste)*
> *1 tsp. oregano or chopped parsley or basil (fresh herbs are best if available)*

1. The evening before, or several hours before serving, wash tomatoes and cut into wedges.
2. Combine remaining ingredients and pour over tomatoes. Stir gently until sugar is dissolved. Cover and refrigerate. Can be served on lettuce as individual salads or served from the bowl using a slotted serving spoon.

Note: This is slightly messy to take along, but goes well with summer picnics and carry-ins.

—Lois Friesen, Towanda, Kansas

Carrot Salad

Makes 8 servings

> **2 lbs. carrots, cooked and sliced**
> **1 green pepper, sliced**
> **1 large onion, sliced**
> **1 can tomato soup**
> **1 cup sugar**
> **3/4 cup vinegar**
> **1 tsp. salt**
> **1 tsp. pepper**

1. Arrange first three ingredients in alternate layers in bowl.
2. Combine remaining ingredients. Heat to boiling. Pour hot liquid over vegetables. Chill before serving.

—Edwina Stoltzfus, Lebanon, Pennsylvania

Baked German Potato Salad

Makes 10–12 servings

> **1 cup bacon, diced**
> **1 cup celery, sliced**
> **1 cup onion, chopped**
> **3 tsp. salt**
> **3 Tbsp. flour**
> **2/3 cup sugar**
> **2/3 cup vinegar**
> **1/2 tsp. pepper**
> **1 1/3 cups water**
> **8 cups potatoes, cooked and sliced**

1. Fry bacon. Drain and return 4 Tbsp. of drippings to skillet. Add all ingredients but bacon and potatoes. Bring to boil. Add bacon and pour over potatoes.
2. Bake at 350° for 30 minutes.

—Rosetta Mast, Clarence, New York

Cold Potato Salad

Makes 12 servings

8-10 medium sized potatoes
4 eggs, hardboiled
3 Tbsp. pickle relish or chopped pickles
½ cup celery, chopped
1-2 Tbsp. onion, chopped
1 cup sugar
2 heaping Tbsp. flour
1 tsp. salt
1 tsp. dry mustard
2 eggs
water
⅔ cup vinegar
½ cup salad dressing

1. Cook potatoes until tender. Dice and set aside.
2. Hardboil eggs. Dice and add to potatoes. Add pickle, celery and onion.
3. Combine sugar, flour, salt and mustard.
4. Beat eggs in a cup. Add water to eggs to equal one cup. Combine water and egg mixture with sugar mixture. Cook in a double boiler until thickened. Add vinegar and bring to boil. Remove from heat. Stir in salad dressing. Pour dressing over potatoes and mix gently. Chill before serving.

—Allie Guengerich, Kalona, Iowa

Shell Macaroni Salad

Makes 4–6 servings

> 2 cups shell macaroni, uncooked
> salt water (used for boiling)
> 5-6 hard boiled eggs, sliced and chilled
> 6-oz. can chunk tuna, chicken, ham, or leftover meat cut in
>   chunks
> 1/2 cup cheese, chunked
> fresh, raw vegetables (tomatoes, peas, carrots, cucumbers, etc.)
>   of desired amount, cleaned and sliced
> salt to taste
> pepper to taste
> 1/8 tsp. garlic or celery salt
> 1/2-1 cup mayonnaise

1. Boil shells 2 minutes in salt water. Let set 10 minutes with lid on. Rinse with cold water. Drain well.
2. Combine remaining ingredients and mix well. Chill.
3. Mix together lightly, noodles and chilled mixture.

Note: All ingredients should be cool before they are combined. Macaroni and eggs can be cooked in the cool of the morning, and the vegetable mixture can chill in the refrigerator.

Prepare salad at least 1/2 hour before serving so flavors can blend.

My children like green grapes with chicken, Swiss cheese with ham, and cherry tomatoes with tuna. Be creative.

—Susan Minteer, Stilwell, Kansas

Rotini Salad

Makes 10–15 servings

> 3/4 cup vinegar
> 3/4 cup water
> 1 cup sugar
> 2 cups mayonnaise
> 1 cup celery, chopped

1 large onion, chopped
1 lb. macaroni (rotini or twist shape, cooked as package directs)
dash of celery seed
dash of salt
dash of turmeric

1. Combine vinegar, water, and sugar in a jar. Shake until sugar is dissolved.
2. Stir mayonnaise until smooth and creamy. Gradually add vinegar mixture.
3. Combine remaining ingredients. Pour dressing over mixture and stir well. Allow to stand at least 6 hours or overnight to absorb liquids.

A great Memorial Day or 4th of July dish.

—Marilyn Forbes, Lutherville, Maryland

Tuna or Salmon Salad

Makes 6–8 servings

1 cup tomato juice
3-oz. package lemon jello
1 package plain gelatin
2 Tbsp. lemon juice or vinegar
3/4 cup mayonnaise
2 7-oz. cans tuna or salmon
3 Tbsp. hot dog relish
1/2 cup celery, chopped
3 Tbsp. green and red pepper, chopped
2 Tbsp. onion, chopped
chopped parsley (optional)

1. Heat tomato juice to boiling. Add jello and gelatin. Stir until dissolved. Add lemon juice or vinegar. Cool.
2. Combine all remaining ingredients and add to jello mixture. Pour into oiled mold. Chill at least 4 hours before serving.
Note: A fish mold is very attractive.

—Margaret Brubacher, Kitchener, Ontario

Tuna Vegetable Salad

Makes 3–4 servings

>**6-oz. can tuna, drained**
>**1/2 cup alfalfa sprouts**
>**1 cup grated carrots**
>**2/3 cup grated cheese**
>**1 small onion, chopped**
>**1/2 cup mayonnaise**
>**lemon and pepper to taste**
>**parsley, chopped**

Combine all ingredients and mix thoroughly. Use in sandwiches, pita bread or on lettuce leaves. Can be broiled as open-face sandwiches until cheese bubbles.

This is an easy, no-cook meal in the hot summer. I started sneaking grated carrots into a more traditional tuna salad several years ago to get my husband to eat some raw vegetables. Now we like it better this way.

In the winter, this makes hot broiled sandwiches that go well with soup.

—Susan Davis, Nashville, Tennessee

Seafood Mold

Makes 25 buffet servings

>**10 1/2-oz. can tomato soup**
>**1/4 cup cold water**
>**1 envelope unflavored gelatin**
>**8-oz. pkg. cream cheese (at room temperature)**
>**1 cup mayonnaise**
>**1/2 cup onion, minced**
>**4-oz. can tiny shrimp**
>**6-oz. can crabmeat**

1. Heat tomato soup to boiling. Dissolve gelatin in cold water and add to soup. Remove from heat.

2. Pour soup over cream cheese. Beat until smooth. Add mayonnaise and onion. Mix well.
3. Remove veins from shrimp. Carefully pick through crabmeat to remove any shell fragments. Stir shrimp and crabmeat into cheese mixture. Pour into a 1-quart mold and refrigerate overnight to set. Serve unmolded with crackers.

Note: I like to mold this in a curved, fish-shaped mold. Unmold. Use olive slice for eye. Surround with watercress.

—Jane Frankenfield, Harleysville, Pennsylvania

Summer Supper Special

Makes 5–6 servings

1 cup uncooked ring macaroni
6$^{1}/_{2}$-oz. can tuna
1 medium onion, minced
1 cup peas (may be frozen or canned)
$^{1}/_{2}$ cup celery, diced
$^{1}/_{2}$ cup cheese cubes
$^{1}/_{3}$ cup vinegar
$^{1}/_{2}$-1 tsp. salt
dash pepper
$^{1}/_{2}$ cup evaporated milk (more milk may be added if you prefer a moister dish)
$^{1}/_{2}$ cup salad dressing or mayonnaise

1. Prepare macaroni according to package instructions. Drain and place in large bowl.
2. Combine macaroni, tuna, onion, peas, celery, and cheese. Toss lightly.
3. Combine remaining ingredients and mix well. Pour over macaroni mixture and stir gently. Refrigerate until serving time.

—Helen Friesen, Butterfield, Minnesota

Chicken and Noodle Green Salad

Makes 4–6 servings

6 oz. medium egg noodles
3 qts. water, boiling
salt
1/2 cup oil
1/4 cup lemon juice
1 1/2 tsp. garlic salt
2 tsp. sugar
1 tsp. dry mustard
1 tsp. rosemary leaves, crumbled
1/2 tsp. pepper
3 cups chicken, cooked and shredded
1/2 cup parsley, chopped
1/2 cup green onions, sliced thin
8 cups spinach leaves, lightly torn

1. Cook noodles in boiling water with salt till noodles are tender, about 8 minutes. Rinse with cold water and drain well.
2. Mix together next 7 ingredients.
3. Place noodles and chicken in large salad bowl. Add dressing mixture and gently mix together. Cover and chill 1–4 hours.
4. Before serving add parsley, onions, and spinach. Mix together lightly until well distributed.

—Erma Martens, Fresno, California

Chicken Vegetable Mold

Makes 12–16 servings

3 envelopes unflavored gelatin
1 1/2 cups frozen orange juice concentrate
20-oz. can crushed pineapple
12 oz. yogurt
1/2 cup mayonnaise
3 cups cabbage, shredded

1 cup carrots, shredded
2 large bell peppers, chopped
24 oz. grapefruit, lemon, or vanilla soda
3 cups cooked, diced chicken (tuna may be substituted)
nuts (optional)

1. Soften gelatin in orange juice, then heat and stir until gelatin is dissolved.
2. Add remaining ingredients except nuts and mix well. Pour into mold and chill until set. Before serving, sprinkle with chopped nuts.

—Geri Hardison, Little Rock, Arkansas

Hot Chicken and Chip Salad

Makes 6 servings

2 cups chicken, cooked and cubed
2 cups celery, thinly sliced
1 cup bread cubes, toasted
$^{1}/_{2}$ cup almonds, toasted and chopped
$^{1}/_{2}$ tsp. salt
2 tsp. onion, grated
1 cup mayonnaise
2 Tbsp. lemon juice
$^{1}/_{2}$ cup cheese, grated
1 cup potato chips, crushed

1. Combine first 8 ingredients. Pile lightly into baking dish. Sprinkle with cheese, and top with chips.
2. Bake at 450° for 10–15 minutes or until bubbly.

—Edna Brunk, Upper Marlboro, Maryland

Taco Salad

Makes 6–8 servings

> *¹/₂-1 lb. ground beef*
> *1 onion, chopped*
> *1 tsp. oregano*
> *¹/₂ tsp. salt*
> *2 cups red kidney beans, cooked*
> *1 head of lettuce, torn up*
> *2 large tomatoes, chopped*
> *2-3 cups corn chips*

1. Brown first 4 ingredients in skillet, then chill.
2. Combine remaining ingredients and add to chilled beef mixture. Toss together and add dressing.

French Dressing

> *1 can tomato soup*
> *¹/₂ cup salad oil*
> *1 onion*
> *¹/₂ cup vinegar*
> *¹/₂ tsp. prepared mustard*
> *²/₃ cup sugar*
> *¹/₂ tsp. paprika*
> *1 tsp. salt*
> *dash of cloves, ground*

Combine all ingredients in a blender.

Mississippi summers are hot! Taco Salad with Cardamom Braid has become a favorite, nutritious, easy-to-prepare, and cool meal to make. It's most often served Sunday noon at our house because we often don't get home from church till 1 or 2 o'clock. Taco Salad is quick. You can have the dressing made, the meat fried, the beans cooked, the tomatoes cut up, and the lettuce washed and drained ahead of time.

—Sarah Ellen Myers, Jackson, Mississippi

Salad Dressing

For Potato, Tuna, and Macaroni Salads, and Deviled Eggs

1/2 cup vinegar
1/2 cup water
2 eggs, well beaten
1 cup sugar
1 Tbsp. flour
1 tsp. salt
1 cup mayonnaise

1. Bring vinegar and water to boil.
2. Beat eggs, sugar, flour, and salt together well and add to vinegar-water mixture. Boil one minute.
3. Stir in mayonnaise until smooth.

—Marilyn Forbes, Lutherville, Maryland

Open Jar Dills

Makes 1 gallon

6 cups water
1 cup vinegar
1/3 cup salt
cucumbers to fill 1 gallon jar
6 dill stems
4-5 garlic buds
1 hot pepper (optional)
1 Tbsp. alum

1. Boil water, vinegar, and salt.
2. Slit cucumbers in middle, about 3 places, and pack in jar. Pour hot water mixture into jar, over the cucumbers. Add remaining ingredients.
3. Allow to set 8-9 days in warm place, covered loosely.

Note: You may use long cucumbers and cut them to fit into the jar. Also, dill seed can be used in place of the dill stems.

—Sharon Baker, Palmer Lake, Colorado

Tomato Dagwood Sandwiches

Bread
Salad dressing
Tomatoes
Sweet peppers
Celery
Cheese

1. Spread salad dressing on as many slices of bread as needed.
2. Place thinly sliced tomatoes over salad dressing.
3. Sprinkle with chopped peppers and celery.
4. Top with sliced cheese.
5. Place under broiler and broil until cheese is bubbly. Serve immediately.

A delicious, easy-to-fix Sunday evening supper!

—Jean Shenk, Mt. Joy, Pennsylvania

Variation:
Add a slice of bacon to each sandwich before broiling.

—Wanda Pannabecker, Bluffton, Ohio

Fried Zucchini

1 large zucchini
salt
1 egg, slightly beaten
1 onion, chopped fine
2 cups cracker crumbs
2 Tbsp. butter

1. Slice zucchini into 1″ thick slices. Salt each piece.
2. Combine chopped onion and cracker crumbs in a small dish. Dip each zucchini slice in the egg, then in the crumbs.
3. Melt butter in large fry pan and allow pan to get moderately hot before adding zucchini. Fry slowly until brown on underside. Flip and brown other side. Add more butter if necessary. Serve when tender.

Note: For this recipe we usually use the larger zucchini and peel them.

Smaller ones can be used and cut diagonally to make the slices larger.

This is our children's favorite way of serving zucchini. They watch them grow to see when they're big enough.

—Verla Fae Haas, Bluesky, Alberta

Rice-Filled Zucchini

Makes 6 servings

> **3 medium zucchini**
> **1 Tbsp. butter**
> **1 small onion, diced**
> **³/₄ cup rice, uncooked**
> **¹/₄ tsp. salt**
> **1³/₄ cups water**
> **³/₄ cup peas**
> **¹/₂ cup milk**
> **¹/₂ cup mozzarella cheese, shredded**
> **¹/₂ cup Velveeta® cheese, shredded**

1. Cut zucchini lengthwise in half. Scoop out and dice centers, leaving ¹/₄" thick shell.
2. In 3-quart pan over medium heat, cook diced zucchini, butter, and onion until tender, stirring occasionally. Add rice, salt, and 1¹/₂ cups water. Heat to boiling. Cover and simmer for 10 minutes. Add peas and simmer 10 more minutes or till liquid is absorbed. Stir in milk, mozzarella cheese, and ¹/₄ cup Velveeta® cheese. Remove from heat.
3. In large skillet heat zucchini halves in ¹/₄ cup water to boiling. Reduce heat, cover, and simmer 5 minutes or till tender-crisp. Salt halves if desired.
4. Fill halves with rice mixture. Sprinkle with remaining Velveeta®. Place back in skillet, cover, and cook over low heat till filling is hot and cheese is melted.

Note: Don't use zucchini that are too old, as the skins will be tough. Don't overcook halves or they get soft and fall apart. Any kind of cheese may be used, but yellow cheese looks more appetizing.

—Bonnie Brechbill, Chambersburg, Pennsylvania

Zucchini-Crusted Pizza

Makes 4–6 servings

> 3¹/₂ *cups coarsely grated zucchini*
> *salt*
> 3 *eggs, beaten*
> ¹/₃ *cup flour*
> ¹/₂ *cup grated mozzarella cheese*
> ¹/₂ *cup grated parmesan cheese*
> 1 *Tbsp. fresh basil leaves, minced or* ¹/₂ *tsp. dried basil*
> *salt and pepper to taste*

1. Salt zucchini lightly and allow to stand for 15 minutes. Squeeze out excess moisture.
2. Combine zucchini with all remaining ingredients and spread onto an oiled 9″ x 13″ baking pan. Bake at 350° for 25–30 minutes until surface is dry and firm.
3. Brush top with oil and broil under moderate heat for 5 minutes.
4. Top with all your favorite pizza toppings. Bake at 350° for 25–30 minutes. Cut into squares and serve.

— *Doreen Snyder, Waterloo, Ontario*

Millet-Squash Casserole

Makes 5–6 servings

> 1 *large onion, chopped*
> 1 *green pepper, chopped, or jar of pimentos*
> ¹/₂ *lb. cheese, grated*
> ³/₄ *cup raw millet*
> ³/₄ *cup whole wheat bread crumbs*
> 4–5 *fresh tomatoes, chopped in blender*
> *herb salt to taste*
> *several squash (chopped into* ¹/₂″ *pieces, enough to loosely fill*
> *9″ × 13″ pan)*

1. Toss together all ingredients until thoroughly mixed.

2. Cover with heavy foil, or self-fitting metal cake pan lid, and bake in oiled pan at 350° for 2 hours.

—*Carolyn Hochstetler, Wellman, Iowa*

Chicken Zucchini Bake

Makes 12–14 servings

1 stick butter
8 oz. seasoned stuffing cubes
5 cups zucchini, cubed
1 tsp. salt
10-oz. can cream of chicken soup
1 cup sour cream
¼ cup milk
4 cups chicken, cooked and cubed

1. Melt butter and mix well with stuffing cubes. Place half of mixture into greased 9″ × 12″ baking dish.
2. Parboil zucchini with salt. Drain and place over crumbs.
3. Combine soup, sour cream, and milk. Mix well. Add chicken and pour over zucchini. Top with remaining stuffing cubes.
4. Bake at 350° for 25 minutes, or 8 minutes at 70% in microwave, turning to cook 8 more minutes if needed.

—*Esther Deal, Fort Wayne, Indiana*

Italian Eggplant Casserole

Makes 4–5 servings

> **1 medium eggplant, peeled and diced**
> **1 medium onion, sliced**
> **salt**
> **water**
> **1 cup shredded cheese**
> **1 cup crushed saltine crackers**
> **2 eggs, beaten**
> **2 strips bacon**

1. Cook eggplant and onion in salt water until tender. Drain.
2. Combine cheese, crackers and eggs. Add to eggplant. Turn into greased casserole. Top with bacon slices. Bake at 350° for 30 minutes.

—Ruth Layman, Newport News, Virginia

Fried Okra

Makes 2 servings

> **15–20 small okra (2″×4″)**
> **cornmeal**
> **oil**

1. Slice okra crosswise into ¼″ slices. Roll in cornmeal.
2. Drop into hot oil. Fry until golden brown and crisp.
Note: Okra should be small and firm. Anything much over 4″ in length tends to be tough, woody and inedible, like chewing on bamboo.

—Susan Davis, Nashville, Tennessee

Escalloped Cabbage

Makes 4 servings

> 2 cups cabbage, shredded
> 1 onion, chopped
> 4 Tbsp. stuffed olives, sliced
> 1½ cups medium white sauce
> 1 cup cracker crumbs, buttered
> ½ cup cheese, grated

1. Cook cabbage and onion in small amount of water for 5 minutes. Drain. Mix with olives and white sauce.
2. Put into 9″×12″ casserole dish in layers, alternating cabbage mixture, crumbs, and cheese. Top with remaining cheese and bake at 325° for 25–30 minutes.

Note: This can be made in a tightly covered skillet over low heat on the top of the stove when it's too hot to turn on the oven.

—Helen Widmer, Wayland, Iowa

Sweet and Sour Carrots

Makes 6–8 servings

> 3 cups carrots
> 1 green pepper, chopped
> 1 onion, chopped
> 1 can tomato soup
> ¾ cup sugar
> ½ cup oil
> ¼ cup vinegar
> 1 tsp. Worcestershire® sauce
> 1 tsp. prepared mustard

1. Cook carrots until tender. Drain and set aside.
2. Combine remaining ingredients. Heat thoroughly. Add carrots. Marinate overnight. Heat well before serving.

—Elizabeth Yoder, Belleville, Pennsylvania

Summer Vegetable Casserole

1 layer (according to size of baking dish) zucchini, peeled
and sliced
1 layer corn
1 layer green beans, lima beans, and broccoli, parboiled
1 layer onions, sliced in rings
1 layer green peppers, sliced in rings
1 layer tomatoes, sliced
1 layer cheese, grated
1 layer bread cubes, coated with melted butter

Bake at 350° for 30 minutes, or till vegetables are soft.

This is a recipe I concocted after someone gave me a zucchini. My family thinks they don't like zucchini, but they loved this dish.

—Loretta Lapp, Kinzers, Pennsylvania

Corn Custard Pie

Makes 6 servings

3 eggs
1 heaping Tbsp. flour
1 cup milk
2 cups corn, fresh or frozen
salt and pepper to taste
2 Tbsp. butter
9" unbaked pie crust

1. Beat eggs and flour. Add milk.
2. Add corn and seasoning.
3. Pour into unbaked pie shell. Dot with butter.
4. Bake at 400° for 20 minutes, then 350° for 25 minutes or until set.

—Edna Keener, Lititz, Pennsylvania

Rice Pilau

Makes 10–12 servings

> 3 Tbsp. butter
> 3 Tbsp. peanut oil
> 1 cup green onion, chopped
> 1 small green pepper, minced
> 3 cups long-grain rice, raw
> 3 cups water
> 3 cups chicken broth
> salt to taste
> 1 cup fresh tomatoes, seeded and diced
> 1/2 cup green olives, sliced
> 1/2 cup almonds, slivered
> 1/4 cup butter

1. Combine butter and peanut oil in skillet. Add onions and green pepper, and sauté. When soft, add rice and sauté 5 more minutes. Add water, broth and salt. Bring to boil, stirring frequently. Reduce heat to low, cover, and simmer 30 minutes.
2. Add tomaotes and olives and remove from heat. Let stand covered for up to 10 minutes.
3. Sauté almonds in butter. Stir into rice just before serving.

—Jane Frankenfield, Harleysville, Pennsylvania

Sesame Noodles

Makes 6–8 servings

1 lb. pasta (extra thin spaghetti, linguine, or fettucini)
¼ cup sesame oil (no substitutions!)
3 Tbsp. soy sauce
¼ tsp. black pepper (fresh ground if possible)
½ tsp. garlic, finely chopped
½ red pepper, diced, or small jar pimentos
¼ cup watercress, chopped

1. Drop pasta into large pot of boiling water. Cook for 3 minutes after water returns to a boil. Add 1 tsp. oil to water.
2. Drain quickly, submerge in cold water, and drain again thoroughly.
3. Mix oil, soy sauce, pepper, and garlic. Immediately pour onto hot pasta. Toss in red pepper and watercress.

Note: Parsley can be substituted for the watercress, but it will change the taste.

—Betsy Beyler, Fairfax, Virginia

Buttermilk and Noodles

Makes 6 servings

8-oz. pkg. noodles, preferably egg noodles
1 qt. buttermilk
½ cup light cream (optional)

1. Boil noodles as directed. Rinse with cold water.
2. Pour buttermilk and cream into large serving bowl. Add noodles to desired consistency, and stir with ladle.
3. Serve and season to taste.

This is a filling dish and delicious on a hot summer's day. This recipe was passed on to me verbally by my mother-in-law.

—Clara Doerksen, Steinbach, Manitoba

Cottage Cheese Delight

Makes 12–15 servings

> ¹/₄ *cup butter, melted*
> 1 *lb. Monterey Jack cheese, shredded*
> 1 *cup milk*
> 1 *cup flour*
> 1 *pt. cottage cheese*
> 6 *eggs, slightly beaten*
> ¹/₄ *cup butter, melted*

1. Spread ¹/₄ cup melted butter over bottom of a 12″ × 7″ baking dish.
2. Combine the remaining ingredients in a bowl.
3. Pour cheese mixture into dish and bake at 375° for 40 minutes, or until golden and set.

This may be served hot or cold, cut in small cubes, and taken to carry-in suppers.

—Charlotte Croyle, Archbold, Ohio

Oven Eggs

Makes 4 servings

> **2 Tbsp. butter**
> **6 large eggs**
> **¹/₃ cup milk**
> **¹/₄ tsp. salt**
> **¹/₈ tsp. pepper**

1. Melt butter in 8″ square pan in 350° oven, and shake pan to distribute evenly.
2. Beat eggs, milk, salt, and pepper until foamy. Pour into pan. Bake at 350° until thickened, but still moist, about 10 minutes.
3. After the first 7 minutes, gently draw a wide spatula across bottom of pan to help form soft curds. (Bits of meat and grated cheese may be added. Timing remains the same.)

Note: It's very important to time this accurately, or eggs will overcook and become rubbery.

This egg recipe reminds me of a story. One day when our youngest, Amy, was in kindergarten, and I was out of town, my husband phoned home from his church office at about the time the school bus should have deposited Amy. A little voice answered, "Hello, Croyles', Amy speaking."

Her daddy explained that he just wanted to make sure she had gotten home all right, then asked casually, "What are you doing, Amy?" "Oh, I'm making an egg." Her innocent answer sent him scurrying home to find her actually frying an egg on the stove, correctly and safely. He then casually explained that cooking on the stove is best done when an adult is there, but that she had done a marvelous job!

If I had my parenting to do all over again, I would begin when the children were very young to collect a recipe file for each one, including our two sons.

—Charlotte Croyle, Archbold, Ohio

Deviled Egg and Ham Casserole

Makes 6 servings

Deviled Eggs

> **6 hard-boiled eggs, halved**
> **2 Tbsp. mayonnaise**
> **1/4 tsp. salt**
> **1/4 tsp. pepper**
> **1/2 tsp. dry mustard**

1. Remove yolks from eggs. Mix yolks well with remaining ingredients.
2. Fill egg halves with yolk mixture.
3. Arrange eggs in greased 10" x 6" x 1½" baking dish.

Sauce

> **1/4 cup butter, melted**
> **1/4 cup flour**
> **2 cups milk**
> **1 cup cheese, grated**
> **1½ cup peas, cooked and drained**
> **1 cup ham, cooked and diced**
> **1/2 cup bread crumbs, coated with 3 Tbsp. melted butter**

1. Blend butter and flour. Add milk. Stir in cheese, peas, and ham. Pour over eggs, and sprinkle with crumbs.
2. Bake at 375° for 15 minutes.

—Rhoda Lind, Ephrata, Pennsylvania

Cheese Souffle

3 Tbsp. minute tapioca
1 tsp. salt
1 cup milk
3/4–1 cup mild cheese, grated
3 egg yolks, beaten until thick and lemon colored
3 egg whites, stiffly beaten

1. Combine tapioca, salt, and milk in pan and cook over medium heat, stirring constantly, until the mixture comes to a boil.
2. Remove from heat. Add cheese and stir until melted.
3. Cool slightly. Add egg yolks and mix well.
4. Gradually add above mixture to the egg whites, folding in thoroughly.
5. Turn into greased 1½ qt. baking dish. Place in pan of hot water and bake at 350° for 50 minutes or until souffle is firm.

My mother usually served this with fresh green beans and tomatoes from the garden.
I often fix it for brunch with fresh fruit and muffins.

—Edna Brunk, Upper Marlboro, Maryland

Reuben Quiche

Makes 4–6 servings

1 cup sauerkraut
1 cup Swiss cheese, grated
1 cup corned beef, cubed or chipped
5 eggs, beaten
3/4 cup milk
1 pie shell, baked

1. Combine first 5 ingredients and pour into pie shell.
2. Bake at 350° for 45–55 minutes.

This is a tasty brunch or supper anytime, but I especially like to serve it with fresh applesauce or sliced tomatoes, making it a great summer dish.

—Edna Brunk, Upper Marlboro, Maryland

Spinach Pie

Makes 6 servings

> 1/2 lb. mild Italian sausage links, chopped
> 3 eggs, slightly beaten
> 10-oz. pkg. frozen chopped spinach, thawed and drained
> 2 cups Swiss or mozzarella cheese, shredded
> 1/3 cup cottage cheese
> 1/4 tsp. salt
> dash pepper
> dash garlic powder
> 1 pie crust, unbaked

1. Cook sausage links until well browned. Drain fat.
2. Combine remaining ingredients in a large bowl. Add sausage and stir.
3. Pour into pie crust. Bake at 375° for 50 minutes or until golden. Let stand 10 minutes before cutting.

—Dorcas Hanbury, Chesapeake, Virginia

Cooked Barbecue Sauce

> 1 cup ketchup
> 1 cup water
> 2 Tbsp. vinegar
> 1 1/2 Tbsp. sugar
> 1/4 tsp. salt
> dash pepper
> 1/8 tsp. chili powder
> 1 Tbsp. Worcestershire® sauce
> 1/4 tsp. Tabasco® sauce
> 1 1/2 Tbsp. onion, grated (optional)
> 1 Tbsp. lemon juice

Combine all ingredients in a saucepan and simmer 10 minutes.
Note: Use on chicken, spare ribs, ham, and pork chops.

**—Vileen Hostetler,
Colorado Springs, Colorado**

Barbecue and Beans

Makes 10–12 servings

> *1 lb. ground beef*
> *1 large onion, chopped*
> *2 1-lb. cans of canned beans*
> *¹/₂ cup catsup*
> *1 Tbsp. Worcestershire® sauce*
> *2 Tbsp. brown sugar*
> *2 Tbsp. vinegar*

1. Brown beef and onions and skim off fat.
2. Add remaining ingredients and mix.
3. Bake at 300°–325° for 1 hour uncovered.

Note: This may also be prepared in a crook-pot, but if the cover is left on the dish tends to get watery.

    Depending on how the dish is used (as main dish, side dish, pot luck, etc. . . .) I vary the amount of meat or beans. The seasoning may also be adjusted for taste.

—**Martha Pauls, Regina, Saskatchewan**

Beef Teriyaki Stir-Fry

Makes 8 servings

> *2 lb. round steak, thawed slighty, cut into thin, diagonal,*
>   *1″ long*
> *1 lb. fresh mushrooms*
> *¹/₄ cup oil (or a bit less)*
> *2 cups cabbage, shredded*
> *16-oz. can bean sprouts, drained*
> *8-oz. can water chestnuts, drained and sliced*

1. Marinate beef for 2 hours in marinade.
2. Sauté mushrooms in hot oil for 2 minutes. Add cabbage and sauté 5 minutes. Add beef and marinade. Stir-fry 5 minutes. Add sprouts and water chestnuts. Heat, then serve.

Marinade

> *¹/₄ cup soy sauce*
> *¹/₄ cup Worcestershire® sauce*
> *¹/₄ cup water*
> *1 Tbsp. vinegar*
> *2 medium onions, sliced*
> *1 tsp. garlic, or 1 clove garlic, diced*
> *³/₄ tsp. ginger, ground*

Combine all ingredients in large skillet.

Note: Zucchini may be substituted for the cabbage. Celery, green and red peppers, and bananas may be added with the vegetables.

—Esther Deal, Fort Wayne, Indiana

Adobo Chicken

Makes 4 servings

> *1 medium chicken fryer, cut in frying pieces*
> *4 segments garlic, well crushed*
> *2 tsp. salt*
> *¹/₃ - ¹/₂ tsp. vinegar*
> *1 tsp. Accent®*
> *2 tsp. soy sauce*
> *dash pepper*

1. Marinate chicken in seasonings about 1 hour, then brown in small amount of fat (1-2 Tbsp.). Add marinade and simmer until done. Water may be added if necessary.
2. Serve with rice. Broth makes good gravy for rice.

Note: Pork can be substituted for chicken.

—Frieda Myers, Lombard, Illinois

Chinese Pepper Steak

Makes 6 servings

> **1 sirloin steak (about 2 lbs.)**
> **¼ cup vegetable oil**
> **1 clove garlic**
> **1 Tbsp. fresh ginger or 1 tsp. ground ginger**
> **3 green peppers, seeded and thinly sliced**
> **2 large onions, thinly sliced**
> **¼ cup soy sauce**
> **1 cup tomato sauce**
> **½ tsp. sugar**
> **6 scallions cut in 1" pieces**
> **6-oz. can water chestnuts, drained**

1. Trim fat from steak. Place in freezer for 1 hour to make slicing easier. Cut into slices ⅛" thick.
2. Heat oil. Add garlic and ginger. Add steak. Cook rapidly 1 minute or until meat is light brown, stirring once or twice. Remove meat from skillet or wok.
3. Add peppers and onions to pan and cook 2 minutes, stirring often. Add soy sauce, tomato sauce, and sugar. Simmer 3-4 minutes.
4. Add meat, scallions, and water chestnuts. Heat thoroughly. Serve with rice.

—**Lois Herr, Quarryville, Pennsylvania**

Maryland Crabcakes

Makes 6 servings

> ½ *cup bread crumbs*
> 1 *egg, beaten*
> 5 *Tbsp. mayonnaise*
> 1 *Tbsp. parsley, chopped*
> 2 *tsp. Worcestershire® sauce*
> 1 *tsp. prepared mustard*
> 1 *tsp. salt*
> ¼ *tsp. white pepper*
> 1 *lb. crabmeat*
> *cracker crumbs*
> *vegetable oil*

1. Mix first 8 ingredients well. Pour over crabmeat, folding in lightly but thoroughly.
2. Form into six cakes. Roll in cracker crumbs.
3. Fry in oil until golden brown (2-3 minutes).

Note: May be served in hamburger buns as sandwiches or served as the main course.

—Etta King, Princess Anne, Maryland

Peach Pie

Makes 6 servings

Crust

> **20 graham crackers**
> **1/2 stick butter or margarine, melted**
> **1/4 cup sugar**

1. Mix ingredients well. Line 9″ pie pan with crumbs, packing firmly. Save small amount for pie topping.
2. Bake at 350° for 5-8 minutes. Cool.

Filling

> **4 peaches, peeled and sliced**
> **1 Tbsp. lemon juice**
> **3/4 cup sugar**
> **dash salt**
> **1 pkg. unflavored gelatin**
> **1/4 cup cold water**
> **1/2 cup hot water**
> **1/2 cup whipping cream**

1. Combine first 4 ingredients. Let stand 15 minutes.
2. Moisten gelatin with cold water; let soften. Add hot water. Combine with peaches.
3. Refrigerate until mixture starts to congeal. Fold in whipped topping. Scoop into pie shell. Top with crumbs. Chill.

—Janet Parthemore, Middletown, Pennsylvania

Streusel Cream Peach Pie

Makes about 6–8 servings

> **4 cups peaches, quartered and peeled**
> **1/2 cup granulated sugar**

¹/₂ tsp. nutmeg
dash salt
1 egg
2 Tbsp. cream or evaporated milk
¹/₂ cup flour
¹/₄ cup brown sugar
2 Tbsp. butter
9″ unbaked pie shell

1. Arrange peaches in pie shell and sprinkle with granulated sugar, nutmeg, and salt.
2. Beat egg and cream. Pour over peaches.
3. Mix flour, brown sugar, and butter until crumbly. Sprinkle over pie.
4. Bake at 425° for 35–45 minutes.

—Esther Heatwole, Rocky Ford, Colorado

Fresh Blueberry Pie

Makes 6–8 servings

5 cups blueberries or huckleberries, washed
1 cup sugar
1 cup water
1 tsp. lemon rind, grated
3 Tbsp. cornstarch
whipped cream
9″ pie shell, baked

1. In saucepan combine 1 cup berries, ³/₄ cup sugar, ³/₄ cup water and lemon rind. Boil.
2. Combine remaining sugar, water, and cornstarch, and stir into the boiling berries. Cook for 1 minute or until clear and thickened. Cool.
3. Place remaining berries in pie shell. Cover with cooled glaze and chill until completely set.
4. Serve with whipped cream.

—C. Kathryn Yoder, Goshen, Indiana

Blueberry Cottage Cheese Pie

Makes 6 servings

Crust

> 1½ cups graham cracker crumbs
> 3 Tbsp. sugar
> ⅓ cup butter, melted

1. Mix ingredients and press mixture firmly and evenly against bottom and sides of 9″ pie plate.
2. Bake at 350° for 10 minutes; then cool.

Filling

> 2 Tbsp. cold water
> 2 Tbsp. lemon juice
> 1 pkg. unflavored gelatin
> ½ cup milk, heated to boiling
> 1 egg
> ⅓ cup sugar
> 2 cups cottage cheese, creamed

1. Blend water, lemon juice, and gelatin in blender on low speed to soften gelatin. Add boiling milk and blend till gelatin is dissolved. Add remaining ingredients and blend at high speed till mixture is smooth and well blended.
2. Pour into cooled crust and chill about 2 hours until set.

Blueberry Glacé

> ¼ cup water
> 2 cups fresh or frozen blueberries
> ¼ cup sugar
> 1½ tsp. cornstarch
> ¼ cup water
> ¼ tsp. cinnamon
> ½ tsp. lemon juice

1. Place ¼ cup water and blueberries in small saucepan. Bring to boil and simmer 3 minutes.

2. Mix sugar and cornstarch in bowl. Add ¼ cup water. Add to blueberry mixture. Add cinnamon. Bring to boil. Boil 1 minute, stirring constantly. Add lemon juice.
3. Cool and pour over chilled cottage cheese mixture.
4. Refrigerate till set.

—*Judith Janzen, Salem, Oregon*

Zucchini Pie

Makes 6 servings

> **3 cups zucchini, coarsely shredded**
> **3 tsp. lemon juice**
> **1 cup sugar**
> **3 Tbsp. flour**
> **1 tsp. cinnamon**
> **1 pie crust, unbaked**
> **2 tsp. butter**
> **1 pie lattice**

1. Combine zucchini and lemon juice in bowl.
2. Stir together sugar, flour, and cinnamon. Add to zucchini. Pour into pie crust. Slice butter evenly on top. Place lattice on very top.
3. Bake at 350° for 45 minutes or till done.

—*Marie Martin, Burr Oak, Michigan*

Cheesecake

Makes 8–10 servings

Crust

> **2¹/₂ cups graham crackers, crushed**
> **²/₃ cup butter, melted**
> **1¹/₂ Tbsp. sugar**
> **1 tsp. cinnamon**

1. Mix all ingredients together.
2. Press on to bottom and sides of 10″ spring form pan.
3. Refrigerate till ready to use.

Filling

> **1 lb. cream cheese**
> **1 cup sugar**
> **¹/₄ cup flour**
> **5 eggs, separated**
> **3¹/₂ Tbsp. lemon juice**
> **1 lemon rind, grated**
> **2 cups sour cream**

1. Beat cheese with sugar until light. Add flour and egg yolks. Beat until smooth. Add lemon juice, rinds, and sour cream. Beat with electric mixer for 10 minutes.
2. Beat egg whites until stiff. Gently fold into cheese mixture.
3. Pour into crust and bake at 325° for 1 hour. Turn off heat and leave in oven for 1 hour. Open oven door and leave in for 1 more hour. (This is necessary to keep the cake from falling.) Remove from oven and cool. Remove sides of pan.

Topping

> **1¹/₂ cups strawberries**
> **¹/₂ cup apple juice**
> **¹/₂ cup sugar**
> **2 Tbsp. cornstarch**
> **2 Tbsp. water**

1. Mix ¹/₂ cup strawberries, apple juice, and sugar in saucepan. Boil.

2. Mix cornstarch with water. Add to fruit mixture. Cook, stirring constantly, till thick and transparent. Add remaining strawberries.
3. Cool and spread on top of cheesecake.

—Lynette Martin, St. Jacobs, Ontario

Peaches 'N Cream Cheese Cake

Makes 1 square cake

> *³/₄ cup flour*
> *1 tsp. baking powder*
> *¹/₂ tsp. salt*
> *3¹/₂-oz. pkg. dry vanilla pudding mix (not instant)*
> *3 Tbsp. butter, softened*
> *1 egg*
> *¹/₂ cup milk*
> *2 cups fresh peaches, sliced*
> *8-oz. pkg. cream cheese, softened*
> *¹/₂ cup sugar*
> *3 Tbsp. peach juice*
> *1 Tbsp. sugar*
> *¹/₂ tsp. cinnamon*

1. Combine first 7 ingredients and beat 2 minutes at medium speed. Pour into greased 9″ cake pan.
2. Place peach slices in single layer on top of batter.
3. Combine cream cheese, ¹/₂ cup sugar, and peach juice in small bowl and beat 2 minutes.
4. Spoon on top of peaches, within 1″ of edge of batter. (Make sure this batter does not touch side of baking dish, or it will bake out over sides). Mix 1 Tbsp. sugar and cinnamon, and sprinkle over top. Bake at 350° for 30–35 minutes.

Note: Bake in 8″ or 9″ square pan. Refrigerate to cool completely, then cut into small squares to take to finger-foods-meal.

I place this recipe with summer because I have sent it with my children when they went swimming with friends.

—Charlotte Croyle, Archbold, Ohio

Never-Fail Cupcakes

Makes 1 dozen

1 egg
¹/₃ cup cocoa
¹/₂ cup shortening
1¹/₂ cups flour
¹/₂ cup sour milk
1 tsp. vanilla
1 tsp. baking soda
1 cup sugar
¹/₂ cup hot water

1. Combine all ingredients in bowl in order given, waiting to mix until last ingredient has been added. Beat well.
2. Pour into cupcake cups.
3. Bake at 350° for 20–25 minutes, till center has no dent in it.
4. Cool and frost with chocolate butter icing.

—Hazel Miller, Hudson, Illinois

Burnt Sugar Cake

Makes 2 8" square cakes

> ¹/₂ **cup sugar**
> ¹/₂ **cup water, boiling**
> ¹/₂ **cup butter**
> 1¹/₂ **cups sugar**
> 2 **eggs, beaten**
> ¹/₂ **cup milk**
> 2 **cups flour**
> 2 **tsp. baking powder**
> ¹/₂ **cup flour**
> 1 **tsp. vanilla**

1. Burn ¹/₂ cup sugar by heating it in a frying pan. Add boiling water to make the syrup. Cool and set aside 3 Tbsp. for frosting.
2. Cream butter and 1¹/₂ cups sugar. Add eggs, milk, flour, and burnt sugar syrup. Stir together. Add baking powder, flour, and vanilla.
3. Bake in two 8" x 8" pans at 350° for 30 minutes.

Burnt Sugar Frosting

> 2 **cups confectioner's sugar**
> ¹/₈ **cup shortening**
> ¹/₈ **cup butter**
> 3 **Tbsp. burnt sugar syrup**
> 1 **tsp. vanilla**
> 2 **Tbsp. cream**

Cream together all ingredients. (Sprinkle chopped walnuts on top if desired).

This old recipe of my mother's is not a light cake. It is very good served with vanilla ice cream at family reunions in July.

—Fern Hostetler, Altoona, Pennsylvania

Chocolate Applesauce Cake

Makes 1 long cake

> ¹/₂ **cup cooking oil**
> 1¹/₂ **cups sugar**
> ¹/₂ **tsp. cinnamon**
> 2 **cups applesauce**
> 2 **eggs**
> 1¹/₂ **tsp. baking soda**
> ¹/₂ **tsp. salt**
> 2 **cups flour**
> 2 **Tbsp. cocoa**

1. Combine all ingredients in bowl and beat well.
2. Pour batter into 9" x 13" pan, and sprinkle with topping.
3. Bake at 350° for 40 minutes.

Topping

> 4 **Tbsp. brown sugar**
> ¹/₂ **cup pecans**
> 1 **cup chocolate chips**

Mix together.

This cake is convenient for outdoor picnics because the icing doesn't melt.

—Elvera Suderman, Newton, Kansas

Chocolate Zucchini Cake

Makes 1 long cake

> ½ cup butter, softened
> ½ cup oil
> 1¾ cups sugar
> 2 eggs
> 1 tsp. vanilla
> ½ cup milk
> ½ tsp. vinegar
> 2½ cups flour
> 4 Tbsp. cocoa
> ½ tsp. baking soda
> ½ tsp. cinnamon
> ½ tsp. cloves
> 2 cups zucchini, finely grated
> 1 cup chocolate chips

1. Cream butter, oil, and sugar. Add eggs, vanilla, and milk which has been mixed with vinegar. Beat well.
2. Mix together dry ingredients. Add to creamed mixture, beating well. Stir in zucchini. Spoon into greased and floured 9″ x 12″ x 2″ pan. Sprinkle chocolate chips over top of cake.
3. Bake at 325° for 40–45 minutes.

Note: This cake stays very moist and tender, so frosting isn't necessary.

—Dorothy Yoder, Hartville, Ohio
—Joanne Hershberger, Columbus, Ohio
—Alma K. Bloss, Jackson, Ohio

Zucchini Cookies

Makes about 4 dozen

> *³/₄ cup butter*
> *1¹/₂ cups sugar*
> *1 egg*
> *1 tsp. vanilla*
> *1¹/₂ cups golden zucchini, grated and peeled*
> *1 tsp. cinnamon*
> *2¹/₂ cups flour*
> *¹/₂ tsp. salt*
> *2 tsp. baking powder*
> *1 cup chocolate chips*
> *1 cup nuts, coarsely chopped*

1. Cream butter and sugar. Beat in egg and vanilla. Mix in zucchini. Stir in remaining ingredients.
2. Drop by heaping teaspoons onto greased and floured cookie sheets.
3. Bake at 350° until cookies are lightly browned, about 15 minutes.
4. Cool on wire rack and sprinkle with powdered sugar if desired.

— Elizabeth Nedwell, Poughkeepsie, New York

Zucchini Cookies

Makes 4 dozen

> *1 cup zucchini, grated*
> *1 tsp. baking soda*
> *1 cup sugar*
> *¹/₂ cup butter or margarine*
> *1 egg, beaten*
> *2 cups flour*
> *1 tsp. cinnamon*
> *¹/₄ tsp. cloves*
> *¹/₂ tsp. salt*
> *1 cup raisins*
> *1 cup nuts, chopped*

1. Mix together first 5 ingredients well. Stir in next 4 ingredients. Blend well. Stir in raisins and nuts.
2. Drop by teaspoonfuls onto cookie sheets.
3. Bake at 375° for 12–15 minutes.

—*Anna Bowman, Ephrata, Pennsylvania*

Frozen Fruit Slush

Makes 15 servings

> **1¹/₂ cups sugar**
> **3 cups water**
> **6-oz. can frozen orange juice concentrate, undiluted**
> **8 ripe bananas, sliced or mashed**
> **20-oz. can (about 1¹/₂ cups) crushed pineapple, including juice**

1. Mix sugar and water and boil for 5 minutes. Cool.
2. Add remaining ingredients and stir.
3. Freeze in ¹/₂-cup portions in individual plastic cups. (Set cups on cookie sheets for ease in placing in freezer.)
4. To serve for a Brunch or a Dessert—thaw at room temperature for about 1 hour. Top each with a dollop of whipped cream and a cherry. Serve in the individual containers the slush was frozen in.
5. To serve for a Snack—eat straight out of the freezer. Unmold easily by wrapping a warm wet cloth around the cup for a short time.

—*Charlotte Croyle, Archbold, Ohio*

Fruit Platz

Makes 24 servings

Crust

> **2 cups flour**
> **3 tsp. baking powder**
> **4 Tbsp. sugar**
> **1/4 cup butter**
> **1 cup cream or evaporated milk**
> **1 egg**

1. Sift and mix first 3 ingredients. Add butter and mix into fine crumbs with fingers. Add cream and egg. Mix well.
2. Pat out on 12″ x 18″ greased baking sheet, pushing up sides.

Filling

> **1 layer of fruit (enough to cover crust)**

Add layer of fruit (any fruit that's in season) and top with Ruebel.

Ruebel

> **1 1/2 cups sugar**
> **3/4 cup flour**
> **1/2 tsp. baking powder**
> **2 Tbsp. butter**
> **cream or evaporated milk**

1. Mix first 3 ingredients well. Rub in the butter, and enough cream to make coarse crumbs, or ruebel.
2. Sprinkle over fruit and bake at 375° for 25–30 minutes, or until top is brown.

Note: If a tart fruit is used, like rhubarb, sprinkle a bit of extra sugar (1–1 1/2 cups) mixed with flour in among the fruit as you put it into the pastry, unless you like a tangy platz.

This is a favorite Mennonite recipe. It's a very versatile dessert and can be anybody's favorite, depending on the fruit you use for the filling. Fresh fruit is always the best but you can also use frozen or canned fruits. Therefore it is very popular at family gatherings, anniversary celebrations, and weddings. Ladies' groups will get together on the morning of the wedding day and quickly bake up several pans of platz, ready to be served "fresh" at the reception.

—Anne Braun, Plum Coulee, Manitoba

Lemon Cheese Dessert

Makes 12–15 servings

30 square graham crackers, crushed fine
¹/₂ cup butter, melted
2 Tbsp. confectioner's sugar
3-oz. pkg. lemon-flavored gelatin
1 cup hot water
1 tsp. vanilla
1 tsp. lemon flavoring
¹/₄ cup lemon juice, freshly squeezed
8 oz. cream cheese
1¹/₂ cups sugar
1 can evaporated milk, chilled

1. Blend crackers, butter and confectioner's sugar well. Press into 9" x 13" pan, saving ¹/₂ cup for top.
2. Scald gelatin in hot water. Add vanilla, flavoring, and lemon juice. Cool, but do not let thicken.
3. Cream cheese and sugar thoroughly. Add gelatin mixture, blending well.
4. Whip evaporated milk and fold into mixture. Pour over crumbs and sprinkle remaining crumbs on top.
5. Refrigerate overnight.

—Viola Stauffer, Milford, Nebraska

Fresh Fruit Cobbler

Makes 6-8 servings

> ¹/₂ *cup sugar*
> 3 *Tbsp. butter*
> ¹/₂ *cup milk*
> 1 *cup flour*
> 1 *tsp. baking powder*
> 1 *tsp. salt*
> 4 *cups fresh berries, or other fruit, cleaned*
> 1¹/₂ *cups sugar*
> 2 *Tbsp. cornstarch*
> 2 *cups water, boiling*

1. Cream sugar and butter. Add milk, flour, baking powder, and salt alternately, beating well.
2. Place fruit in bottom of 8″ x 12″ greased baking pan. Pour dough over fruit, spreading out evenly with spoon.
3. Mix sugar and cornstarch. Sprinkle over dough. Pour water over top.
4. Bake in preheated oven at 350° for 35-40 minutes.
5. Serve warm or cool with ice cream.

Note: This cobbler is quite juicy. May be made with frozen fruit also.

—Doris Schrock, Goshen, Indiana

Peach Cobbler

Makes 8-10 servings

> 3 *cups peaches, sliced*
> ¹/₃ *cup granulated sugar*
> ¹/₄ *cup brown sugar*
> *dash nutmeg*
> *dash cinnamon*
> 1 *stick butter*
> ¹/₂ *cup granulated sugar*
> ³/₄ *cup flour*
> 2 *tsp. baking powder*

³/₄ cup milk

1. Mix and set aside first 5 ingredients.
2. Preheat oven to 350°, and melt butter stick in 9" x 13" baking dish.
3. Stir together remaining ingredients to make batter. Pour batter over melted butter, but do not stir. Spoon sugared peaches over batter.
4. Bake at 350° for 45 minutes.
5. Serve warm with ice cream.

— *Judith Pritchard, Taylors, South Carolina*

Jiffy Peach Pudding

Makes 4-6 servings

> **1 cup flour**
> **2 tsp. baking powder**
> **2 tsp. sugar**
> **¹/₄ tsp. salt**
> **2 Tbsp. butter**
> **¹/₂ cup milk**
> **1¹/₂ cups peaches, peeled and diced**
> **1 cup brown sugar, packed tightly**
> **1¹/₂ cups water, boiling**
> **2 Tbsp. butter**

1. Sift first four ingredients together in a bowl. Add 2 Tbsp. butter and cut in finely. Stir in milk and peaches. Spoon into greased 1¹/₂ qt. casserole dish.
2. Combine brown sugar, water, and 2 Tbsp. butter. Mix well.
3. Pour over batter in casserole dish and bake 40 minutes, or until pudding rises to top and is golden brown.

Note: Apples or other fresh fruit can be substituted for peaches.

— *Violet Good, Petersburg, Ontario*

Peach Bavarian Souffle

Makes 8 servings

> *3 peaches, peeled and chopped*
> *¼ cup lemon juice*
> *6 eggs, separated*
> *3 pkgs. unflavored gelatin*
> *1 cup sugar*
> *1 tsp. vanilla*
> *1 cup whipping cream, unsweetened*
> *vanilla cookies, crushed*
> *whipped cream, sweetened*
> *peaches, sliced*

1. Attach 3″ high foil collar (greased inside) around top edges of 1½ quart soufflé dish.
2. In blender puree enough peaches to measure 2 cups, adding lemon juice while pureeing to prevent darkening.
3. Beat egg yolks until light. Beat in 1 cup peach puree.
4. In saucepan, combine gelatin and ¼ cup sugar. Add peach-yolk mixture. Place over low heat and stir until gelatin dissolves, about 5 minutes. Remove from heat. Stir in remaining peach puree and vanilla.
5. Chill, stirring occasionally, until mixture mounds when dropped from spoon.
6. Beat egg whites till foamy. Gradually add remaining ¾ cup sugar, beating until stiff but not dry. Fold into chilled peach mixture. Fold in whipped cream. Turn into prepared souffle dish.
7. Chill till firm, 3-4 hours.
8. Remove collar. Press cookie crumbs around sides of souffle. Garnish top with dollops of whipped cream and peach slices.

— Ina Bachman, Glendale, Arizona

Apricot Pudding

Makes 6 servings

> $^1/_2$ **lb. dried apricots**
> **1 cup sugar**
> **4 cups water**
> **3 Tbsp. tapioca**
> **1 pkg. orange gelatin**
> $^1/_4$ **tsp. salt**
> $^1/_2$ **cup whipping cream**

1. Cook apricots till tender. Add sugar to pulp.
2. Boil water. Add tapioca and cook till clear. Add gelatin and salt. Stir till dissolved.
3. Remove from heat and add apricot pulp.
4. Chill thoroughly. Garnish with whipped cream.

—Mrs. Abram Groff, Strasburg, Pennsylvania

Apple Dumplings

Makes 6–8 servings

> **5 cups flour**
> **2$^1/_2$ Tbsp. baking powder**
> **2 tsp. salt**
> $^3/_4$ **cup plus 1 Tbsp. oil**
> **1$^2/_3$ cups milk**
> **9 baking apples, peeled, cored, and halved**
> **1$^1/_2$ Tbsp. sugar**
> **sprinkle of cinnamon, per half**
> **pat of butter, per half**

1. Sift together flour, baking powder, and salt. Add oil and milk. Stir with fork until dough can be formed into a ball.
2. Divide dough into 18 portions. Holding one portion at a time, center an apple half on it, and fill core hollow of apple with $^1/_4$ tsp. sugar, cinnamon, and butter. Form dough to completely cover apple. Place top up

in baking pan.

3. Bake at 375° for 40–50 minutes till dumpling is brown and apple is soft.
4. Serve hot from oven with milk.

Yellow transparent apples remain our favorite, so any cool summer evening when they're in season, apple dumplings are in order.

—Ruth Liechty, Goshen, Indiana

Baked Rice with Raisins

Makes 6–8 servings

> **2 cups rice, dry**
> **6 eggs, beaten**
> **1½ qts. milk**
> **1½ tsp. vanilla**
> **1½ cups sugar**
> **1–1½ cups raisins, soaked in water**

1. Cook rice according to package directions.
2. Combine eggs, milk, vanilla and sugar. Add rice and drained raisins. Mix well.
3. Pour mixture into baking dish and bake at 350° for 40–45 minutes till mixture is golden brown.
4. Remove from oven and cool.

—Paul Nedwell, Poughkeepsie, New York

Mother's American Cream

Makes 8–10 servings

> **1 qt. milk**
> **3 eggs, separated**
> **16 Tbsp. sugar**
> **2 pkgs. plain gelatin**
> **¼ cup and 1 tsp. water**
> **1 tsp. vanilla**

1. Heat milk to steaming. Add beaten egg yolks with 7 Tbsp. sugar. Stir and heat slightly. Remove from heat.
2. Soak 2 Tbsp. gelatin in water, and heat until dissolved. Add to milk mixture.
3. Mix 9 Tbsp. sugar with beaten egg whites. Add to mixture. Add vanilla and stir well. Chill.
4. Serve with red and black raspberries on top, or any fresh fruit, sliced.

—Martha Yake, Lititz, Pennsylvania

Yogurt Bars

Makes 6 popsicles

> **8 oz. plain yogurt**
> **8-10 oz. fruit, any kind**

1. Blend yogurt for 15 seconds.
2. Add fruit and blend till desired smoothness.
3. Pour into popsicle molds and freeze.

—Janet Yoder, Phoenix, Arizona

Fudgesicles

Makes 12 popsicles

> **3³/₄-oz. pkg. chocolate instant pudding**
> **2¹/₂ cups milk**

Mix in blender. Pour immediately into molds and freeze.

— **Janet Yoder, Phoenix Arizona**

Homemade Vanilla Ice Cream

Makes 10-12 servings

> **4-5 eggs**
> **1¹/₄ cup granulated sugar**
> **³/₄ cup brown sugar**
> **¹/₂ tsp. salt**
> **1 Tbsp. vanilla**
> **1 pt. whipping cream**
> **¹/₂ gal. whole milk (approx.)**

1. Pour small amount boiling water into ice cream freezer to scald the can.
2. Beat eggs until thick and light in color. Gradually add sugars while continuing to beat. Add salt and vanilla.
3. Whip cream and add milk to fill line, or 1³/₄″ from top of can. Freeze in ice cream freezer.

Note: To make peppermint ice cream, add ¹/₂ tsp. peppermint extract and several drops of green food coloring, or you can add crushed peppermint stick candy left over from Christmas.

We usually make this in the summer on a Sunday evening and invite another family over to share it with us. We serve it with popcorn and a variety of toppings.

— **Jan Brubacher, Mt. Pleasant, Pennsylvania**

Powdered Milk Ice Cream

Makes 5 quarts

3 pkgs. unflavored gelatin
½ cup cold water
6 eggs
3 cups sugar
2 tsp. vanilla
¼ tsp. salt
2 cups milk, made as directed on dry milk pkg.
4 cups cream, made by doubling amount of dry milk (4 cups cold water; 2⅔ cup dry milk)
4 cups milk, made as directed on dry milk pkg.

1. Soften gelatin in ½ cup cold water. Place over low heat to dissolve, stirring occasionally.
2. Beat eggs. Add sugar, vanilla, salt, and 2 cups milk. Add dissolved gelatin and mix well. Add cream and 4 cups milk. Mix well.
3. Refrigerate until ready to use or start cranking immediately.

Note: Ice cream gets done faster if mix has been refrigerated.

—Norma Slagell, Kalamazoo, Michigan

Easy Soft Ice Cream

Makes 1 gallon

> **2 pkgs. gelatin**
> **¹/₂ cup cold water**
> **5 cups milk**
> **2 cups sugar**
> **2 tsp. vanilla**
> **1 tsp. salt**
> **3 cups cream**

1. Soak gelatin in water.
2. Heat milk, but do not boil. Remove from heat. Add gelatin, sugar, vanilla, and salt. Cool.
3. Add cream. Chill 5–6 hours.
4. Freeze in freezer.

—Mary Ella Martin, Akron, Pennsylvania

Fruit Medley Ice Cream

Makes 1 gallon

> **6-oz. can lemonade, frozen**
> **6-oz. can orange juice, frozen**
> **2 cups water**
> **2 large bananas, mashed**
> **2 cups sugar**
> **1 cup heavy cream**
> **3 cups milk**
> **1 1-lb., 14-oz. can apricots, drained and chopped**

1. Mix together first 7 ingredients. Beat well. Stir in apricots.
2. Pour into gallon freezer can, freezing as for homemade ice cream.

—Maxine Miller, Wakarusa, Indiana

Blender Milkshake

1 cup cold water, or fruit juice
sugar to taste
¹/₂ tsp. vanilla
6 heaping Tbsp. powdered milk (full cream powdered milk if
*   available)*
1–1¹/₂ cups fresh fruit, or cocoa
1 tray ice cubes, crushed

1. Blend first 4 ingredients.
2. Add fruit or cocoa. Slowly add ice cubes and blend till smooth and thick.

We discovered this recipe while working in Bangladesh where few Western "goodies" were available. My first reaction was "Yuck! Water and powdered milk to make a good, thick milkshake?" But because so little was available, we tried it. We were pleasantly surprised.

Now milkshakes, popcorn, and cheese and crackers are our Sunday night sup-per—eaten sitting around a tablecloth on the living room floor.

—Carolyn Yoder, Mbabane, Swaziland

Finger Jello

2¹/₂ envelopes plain gelatin
1 cup cold water
6-oz. pkg. fruit-flavored gelatin
1 cup cold water
¹/₄ cup sugar (optional)
¹/₂ cup cold water

1. Combine plain gelatin and 1 cup water. Let stand.
2. Mix fruit-flavored gelatin, 1 cup water, and sugar. Bring to a boil. Take off heat. Add ¹/₂ cup water and combined plain gelatin water.
3. Pour into flat bottomed dish, 11″ x 9″ x 1¹/₂″. Cool.
4. When set, cut into squares.

For children's parties I use small cookie cutters. The "scraps" are eaten later. Ideal for picnics when a cold dish is needed. Grown-ups enjoy it too.

—Rhoda Lind, Ephrata, Pennsylvania

Tofu Peanut Butter Spread

1 cup tofu
1/4-1/2 cup peanut butter (smooth)
1 1/2-2 bananas
1/2 tsp. vanilla

1. Blend all ingredients in blender till smooth.
2. Spread on bread and serve immediately.

Note: If you want to save it for later, add lemon juice to keep it from turning dark.

   Also, try more tofu and use it as a dressing for apple salad.

   This is a favorite lunch for the kids in hot weather. Sometimes they want the bread spread again after they have licked off the tofu.

—Jane Yoder-Short, Battle Ground, Indiana

Vegetable Dip

1 cup sour cream
1 cup mayonnaise
1 Tbsp. dry onion flakes or raw onion, chopped
3/4 Tbsp. dill weed
1 Tbsp. chives (dried)
3/4 Tbsp. seasoned salt
1 tsp. Beau Monde® seasoning (optional)

Combine all ingredients. Mix well. Allow to stand for several hours in refrigerator. Serve with raw vegetables.

—Wilma Cender, Goshen, Indiana

Cheese Ball

Makes 1 cheese ball

> *1 lb. medium or sharp cheddar cheese*
> *2 Tbsp. red and green peppers, finely chopped*
> *2 Tbsp. onions, grated*
> *1 Tbsp. Worcestershire® sauce*
> *1 Tbsp. lemon juice*
> *8-oz. pkg. cream cheese, softened*
> *2 Tbsp. parsley, chopped*
> *2 Tbsp. mayonnaise*
> *crushed walnuts*

1. Mix all ingredients together well, except walnuts. Shape into ball and roll in crushed walnuts.
2. Place on large plate and surround with grapes, other fruit sections, and crackers.

Note: Room temperature cheeses mix and mold best.

—Margaret Brubacher, Kitchener, Ontario

Dried Beef Pinwheels

> *3-oz. pkg. cream cheese, softened*
> *1 tsp. horseradish*
> *dash Worcestershire® sauce*
> *1 Tbsp. onion, grated*
> *¹/₄ lb. dried beef, or ham*

1. Blend cream cheese, horseradish, Worcestershire® sauce, and onion until of spreading consistency.
2. Carefully separate beef or ham slices and spread with cheese mixture. Roll as for jelly roll and fasten with toothpicks. Chill. Slice into ¹/₂″ slices before serving.

—Dorothy Yoder, Hartville, Ohio

Tea Lemonade

Makes about 6 quarts

> **2 cups sugar (or less)**
> **5 cups water**
> **1 large handful garden tea**
> **1 cup lemon juice**
> **1 cup orange juice**
> **water**

1. Boil sugar in 5 cups water. Pour over garden tea. Cover and steep for 1 hour.
2. Remove tea. Add juices. Refrigerate.

Note: This makes a concentrate which must be diluted with 2 parts water to 1 part concentrate.

I freeze this concentrate and we enjoy it even after the fresh tea is finished.

—Elaine Gibbel, Lititz, Pennsylvania

Grape Cooler

Makes 10–12 servings

> **12-oz. can frozen grape juice concentrate**
> **4 cups cold water**
> **¹/₄-¹/₂ cup lime juice (3–4 limes)**
> **2 small bottles ginger ale**
> **lime slices**

1. Stir well all ingredients except ginger ale. Add ginger ale just before serving. Stir gently.
2. Garnish with lime slices.

—Maxine Miller, Wakarusa, Indiana

Fall

Take out the window screens. Bring in the broccoli. The leaves and children are holding their final outdoor riots. The corn stalks have finished propping up their riches. Frost creeps over the last tomatoes on the terrace and browns the window box gardens.

Feast on cool days with blazing skies. Finish off a walk downtown with a warm bowl of soup. The oven is bursting with warmth and pumpkins baking.

Stir up some Yeast Corn Bread. (It dresses up well with apple butter.) Try a Chinese Vegetable Medley with your Thanksgiving fowl. It's a zesty time with food to match.

For the earth brings forth fruit of herself; first the blade, then the ear, after that the full corn in the ear.

— Mark 4:28

Pumpkin Yeast Bread

Makes 2 loaves

> ¹/₂ cup lukewarm water
> 2 tsp. sugar
> 2 pkgs. dry yeast
> ¹/₄ cup sugar
> ¹/₄ cup molasses
> 2 tsp. salt
> 1 tsp. cinnamon
> 1 tsp. ginger
> 1 tsp. nutmeg
> 1 cup canned pumpkin
> 2 eggs, beaten
> ¹/₂ cup oil
> 1 cup milk, scalded and cooled to lukewarm
> 8 cups flour
> 1 cup raisins

1. Dissolve sugar in water. Sprinkle yeast over water and allow to stand 10 minutes.
2. Combine sugar, molasses, salt, spices, pumpkin and eggs. Add to yeast mixture.
3. Stir in oil, milk and half of flour. Gradually add remaining flour and raisins. Knead until smooth and elastic. Place in greased bowl and cover. Allow to rise until double—about 1¹/₂ hours. Punch down and let rise again (1¹/₂ hours). Shape into 2 loaves. Place in loaf pans and let rise. Bake at 375° for 45–50 minutes.

Note: This is delicious served with apple butter and mint tea.

— *Anna Mary Brubacher, Kitchener, Ontario*

Dilly Bread

Makes 1 loaf

> **1 pkg. dry yeast**
> **¼ cup warm water**
> **1 cup creamed cottage cheese, warmed**
> **1 Tbsp. onion, minced**
> **2 Tbsp. sugar**
> **2 tsp. dill seed**
> **¼ tsp. soda**
> **1 tsp. salt**
> **1 egg, slightly beaten**
> **2 cups flour or enough for stiff dough**

1. Dissolve yeast in warm water.
2. Combine cheese, onion, sugar, dill, soda, salt and egg. Mix well. Add yeast dissolved in water.
3. Stir in flour. Set aside and allow to rise until doubled. Punch down and let rise again. Shape into loaf and place in greased coffee can. Let rise until doubled. Bake at 350° for 40–50 minutes. Bread looks like large mushroom when done.

—Lorna Sirtoli, Cortland, New York

Apple Muffins

Makes 10 muffins

> **½ cup sugar**
> **¼ cup margarine**
> **1 egg, beaten**
> **2¼ cups flour**
> **3½ tsp. baking powder**
> **½ tsp. salt**
> **½ tsp. cinnamon**
> **1 cup milk**
> **1 cup apples, finely chopped**
> **2 Tbsp. sugar**

1. Cream sugar and shortening. Add egg.
2. Sift together flour, baking powder, salt and ¼ tsp. cinnamon. Add alternately with milk. Fold in chopped apples. Fill greased muffin tins ¾ full.
3. Mix 2 Tbsp. sugar with remaining cinnamon. Sprinkle over muffins. Bake at 400° for 20–25 minutes. Allow to stand a minute or two before removing from pan.

—*Mrs. Harold Eshleman, Harrisonburg, Virginia*

Cream of Broccoli Soup

Makes 4–6 servings

> **2 Tbsp. celery, chopped**
> **¼ cup onion, chopped**
> **¼ cup butter**
> **2–3 Tbsp. flour**
> **salt to taste**
> **pepper to taste**
> **1 bay leaf, or herb of your choice**
> **3 cups milk or half and half**
> **3 cups broccoli, cooked**

1. Sauté celery and onions in butter, in heavy saucepan until transparent.
2. Stir in flour, salt, pepper, and herbs. Add milk gradually, stirring constantly. Bring to boil. Simmer and stir a few minutes. Add broccoli, and heat till hot and bubbly.

The same recipe can be used with any of your favorite vegetables: spinach, chard, peas, cauliflower, carrots, or tomatoes.

—*Lorraine Martin, Dryden, Michigan*

Chicken Broccoli Soup

Makes 3 servings

> **2–3 cups fresh or frozen broccoli, chopped**
> **10-oz. can cream of chicken soup**
> **1 cup chicken, cooked and diced**
> **1 soup can of water**
> **¹/₈ tsp. thyme**
> 1. Combine all ingredients in 2-quart saucepan.
> 2. Bring to boil over medium heat. Cover and simmer 5 minutes.

— Maretta Buller, Salida, Colorado

Potato Soup

Makes desired servings

> **1 potato per person**
> **¹/₈ tsp. salt per potato**
> **¹/₂ cup milk per potato**
> **1 tsp. butter per potato**
> **chopped parsley, as desired**

1. Peel and dice potatoes. Cook in as little water as possible. Add salt.
2. When soft, pour off remaining water. Add milk and butter. Heat almost to boiling point. Stir in parsley.

Note: Chopped onion or leeks cooked with potato add flavor, if desired.

Leftover mashed potatoes are excellent base for potato soup. Add milk to desired consistency. Add parsley and butter as desired.

Our family frequently had potato soup the evening of the day we harvested the year's supply of potatoes. Father would turn up the potatoes with a one-horse plow. We would uncover them with a rake or hoe. The whole family had to help pick them up and haul them into a bin in the basement. This was a back-breaking job, and often the wind was brisk and chilly. Good, hot potato soup seemed to be just the right dish to climax the day.

— Lorraine Roth, Kitchener, Ontario

Pumpkin Soup

Makes 8–10 servings

> **1 soup bone or ³/₄ lb. hamburger**
> **2 qts. water**
> **salt to taste**
> **pepper to taste**
> **¹/₄ tsp. thyme**
> **1 clove garlic, chopped**
> **1 onion, chopped**
> **2–3 cups pumpkin, cooked and mashed in blender**
> **2 cups potatoes, cooked and mashed**

1. Cook first 7 ingredients together until meat is tender.
2. Add pumpkin and potatoes. Heat for 5–10 minutes.

I learned to eat and make this in Jamaica. It's a good way to take advantage of all that vitamin A lying around in the fall.

— Twila Brunk, Toana, Virginia

Pumpkin Shell Fruit Salad

Makes 4–6 servings

> **1 small pumpkin, washed**
> **2 cups apples, peeled and chopped**
> **1 cup raisins**
> **1 cup pecans, chopped**
> **1/3 cup sugar**
> **1 tsp. lemon juice**
> **1/4 tsp. cinnamon**
> **1/4 tsp. nutmeg**
> **1 cup dried mixed fruit (apricots, dates, etc.) (optional)**

1. Preheat oven to 350°.
2. Slice off top of pumpkin for a lid. Scrape out seeds.
3. Combine remaining ingredients and pour into pumpkin. Return lid to pumpkin.
4. Bake on cookie sheet for 1–2 hours till apples are tender.
5. Serve from the shell, spooning some pumpkin with each portion. Top with sour cream if desired.

Note: This can be served hot or cold with roast pork, ham or poultry, or even as an appetizer.

— Ginny Birky, Cortez, Colorado

Fruit Salad

Makes 6 servings

> **1 cup sugar**
> **1 1/2 Tbsp. flour**
> **1 egg, beaten**
> **2 cups milk**
> **3 apples, chopped**
> **3 oranges, chopped**
> **1 cup raisins**
> **1 cup pecans, chopped**
> **1 cup bananas, sliced**

1. Combine sugar and flour. Add beaten egg and milk. Stir over medium heat until thickened. Cool.
2. Combine apples, oranges, raisins, and pecans. Pour dressing over fruit. Chill. Add bananas just before serving.

—Ethel Weaver, Blue Ball, Pennsylvania

Pasta Salad

Makes 8 servings

> 1 lb. pasta (3-color spirals or any other shape)
> 1–2 cups broccoli florets, blanched
> 1 tomato, chopped
> 1 cup cucumber, chopped
> 1 cup zucchini, sliced or cubed
> ¹/₂ cup carrots, thinly sliced
> 1 cup Italian dressing, bottled or homemade
> black olives, sliced

1. Cook pasta until tender but not mushy. Drain, then run cold water over it.
2. Place pasta in large bowl. Add your choice of vegetables for color and flavor variety. Toss lightly.
3. Mix in dressing. Chill well (overnight, if possible) so flavors can mingle. Garnish with black olive slices.

I probably prepare this salad most frequently during those seasons when lettuce is expensive and variety in meals is often lacking. Actually, it's good anytime!

—Gloria L. Lehman, Blacksburg, Virginia

Eggplant and Pasta Salad

Makes 3 quarts

> 1 large eggplant, peeled
> salt
> ³/₄ cup olive oil
> ³/₄ cup onion, chopped
> 2 garlic cloves, minced
> 2¹/₂ cups tomatoes, cut in ¹/₂" cubes
> 2 cups cooked pasta
> ³/₄ cup stuffed olives, sliced
> 3 Tbsp. lemon juice
> ³/₄ tsp. salt
> ¹/₈ tsp. pepper

1. Slice eggplant into ¹/₂" slices. Sprinkle with salt. Let stand for 10 minutes. Press liquid from slices. Cut eggplant into ¹/₂" cubes.
2. Heat ¹/₄ cup of the olive oil in skillet. Sauté eggplant, onion and garlic for 10 minutes or until tender. Cool to room temperature.
3. Combine remaining olive oil, tomatoes, pasta, olives, lemon, salt and pepper. Add to cooled eggplant mixture. Mix well. Cover and chill, stirring occasionally.

—Viola King, Hesston, Kansas

Baked Acorn Squash

> acorn squash
> light cream
> salt and pepper

1. Prepare 1 squash for each person to be served. Warm squash. Cut in half and clean cavity.
2. Set squash halves in a pan of boiling water. Fill the cavity of each squash with cream. Sprinkle with salt and pepper. Bake at 400° for 60 minutes or until soft. To eat, mix squash and cream together in the squash shell.

—Carolyn Hochstetler, Wellman, Iowa

Pepper Cabbage

Makes 12 servings

> ³/₄ *cup sugar*
> ¹/₂ *cup vinegar*
> 1 *tsp. celery seed*
> ¹/₂ *cup water*
> 2 *tsp. salt*
> 2 *lb. head of cabbage, chopped fine*
> 2 *green peppers, chopped fine*
> 2 *red peppers, chopped fine*

Combine first 5 ingredients well. Add vegetables. Mix thoroughly.

—Ella Mae Eby, Pennsville, New Jersey

Broccoli Casserole

Makes 8–10 servings

> 2 *packages frozen, chopped broccoli*
> 3 *cups crackers, crushed*
> 2 *Tbsp. butter*
> ¹/₄ *cup mayonnaise*
> 1 *can cream of mushroom soup*
> ³/₄ *cup cheese, grated*
> 2 *Tbsp. onion, chopped*

1. Cook broccoli until tender. Drain.
2. Line bottom of a 9″x13″ baking pan with 2 cups cracker crumbs. Cover crumbs with broccoli. Dot with 1 Tbsp. butter.
3. Combine mayonnaise, soup, cheese, and onion. Pour over broccoli. Sprinkle with remaining crumbs and dot with remaining butter. Bake at 350° for 60 minutes.

—Mrs. Lewis Heatwole, Elida, Ohio

Scalloped Cabbage

Makes 6 servings

> **3 quarts cabbage, chopped**
> **1½ quarts water**
> **1 Tbsp. salt**
> **⅓ cup margarine**
> **¼ cup flour**
> **salt and pepper to taste**
> **1⅓ cups milk**
> **1⅓ cups cheese, grated**
> **2⅔ cups soft bread crumbs**

1. Combine cabbage, water, and salt. Cook 5 minutes. Drain. Turn into a 2-quart casserole.
2. Melt 3 Tbsp. margarine in saucepan. Add flour and stir until smooth. Season. Gradually add milk. Cook slowly, stirring constantly, for 5 minutes. Remove from heat. Add cheese. Pour over cabbage.
3. Melt remaining margarine. Add bread crumbs. Toss lightly. Sprinkle over casserole. Bake at 350° for 20 minutes.

—*Edwina Stoltzfus, Lebanon, Pennsylvania*

Sweet-Sour Red Cabbage

Makes 8–10 servings

> **4 large apples, peeled, cored, and chopped**
> **1 large onion, chopped**
> **¼ cup margarine**
> **1 medium red cabbage, shredded**
> **½ cup water**
> **½ cup dark corn syrup**
> **⅓ cup vinegar**
> **2 Tbsp. margarine**
> **salt to taste**
> **pepper to taste**

1. Combine apples and onion in margarine and cook for 10 minutes. Add cabbage and water. Cook 20 more minutes, adding more water if necessary.
2. Add syrup and vinegar. Cook 5 minutes longer.
3. Just before serving, add butter, salt, and pepper.

— *Rosetta Mast, Clarence, New York*

Chinese Vegetable Medley

Makes 6–8 servings

> **1 large bunch broccoli, separated into florets, tough stems**
>   **discarded**
> **¹/₂ medium head cauliflower, separated into florets**
> **4 medium carrots, cut diagonally into 1″ chunks**
> **2 Tbsp. peanut oil**
> **1 slice fresh ginger, size of a quarter**
> **1 clove garlic**
> **1 cup chicken broth (preferably homemade)**
> **1 Tbsp. soy sauce**
> **¹/₄ cup cold water**
> **salt and pepper to taste**

1. Clean and cut vegetables.
2. Heat oil in wok or large frying pan. Add ginger and garlic. Fry until browned. Discard ginger and garlic.
3. Add vegetables to oil. Stir-fry over high heat for 3 minutes. Add chicken broth and soy sauce. Cover and cook over medium heat 3 minutes more.
4. Dissolve cornstarch in water. Add to vegetables. Cook about 1 minute more until sauce is thickened and glossy. Season to taste. Fresh bean sprouts and sliced water chestnuts can be added before thickening, if desired.

Note: If using canned chicken broth and supermarket-type soy sauce, taste carefully to avoid oversalting. Our family likes this vegetable with our Thanksgiving turkey dinner.

— *Jane Frankenfield, Harleysville, Pennsylvania*

Mother's Potato Casserole

Makes 8 servings

> **1 pt. sour cream**
> **1 cup cheddar cheese, grated**
> **1 Tbsp. onion, finely chopped**
> **salt to taste**
> **10-oz. can cream of chicken soup**
> **½ cup butter, melted**
> **9 potatoes, cooked and grated**
> **½ cup cornflakes or bread crumbs**
> **2 Tbsp. butter, melted**

1. Mix together first 6 ingredients. Add potatoes.
2. Mix cornflakes and 2 Tbsp. butter. Spread evenly on top of potato mixture.
3. Bake at 350° for 1 hour uncovered.

This is a recipe I brought to Mexico, which makes me feel like I'm at Sunday dinner at Mother's.

—Gem Miller, Coyoacan, Mexico

Rice Casserole

Makes 6 servings

> **1 cup dry rice**
> **3 Tbsp. butter**
> **1 green pepper, chopped**
> **1 medium onion, chopped**
> **1 can cream of mushroom soup**
> **1 can beef broth**
> **1 cup mushrooms**

1. Cook rice according to package instructions.
2. Melt butter. Add rice, pepper and onion. Sauté until pepper and onion are soft.

3. Combine rice mixture with remaining ingredients. Stir gently. Turn into casserole and bake at 350° for 60 minutes. Stir once after ½ hour of baking time. Allow to stand several minutes before serving.

—Elizabeth Nedwell, Poughkeepsie, New York

Baked Tomato Rarebit

Makes 6 servings

> *3 cups fresh bread crumbs*
> *1½ cups cheddar cheese, grated*
> *2 eggs, beaten well*
> *½ tsp. dry mustard*
> *1½ tsp. salt*
> *2 cups stewed tomatoes*
> *4–5 slices bacon, fried crisp*

1. Arrange alternate layers of bread and cheese in buttered casserole dish. Pour eggs over top. Sprinkle with seasonings. Cover with tomatoes and let stand at least 10 minutes.
2. Bake at 350° for 30–35 minutes.
3. Top with bacon.

—Edwina Stoltzfus, Lebanon, Pennsylvania

Zucchini Curry

Makes 6–8 servings

>1 Tbsp. margarine
>1 small onion, chopped
>1 tsp. curry powder (more or less to taste)
>1 tsp. dry mustard
>1 tsp. turmeric
>3/4 tsp. ground cumin
>3/4 tsp. ground coriander
>1/2 tsp. salt
>3 6–8" zucchini, thinly sliced
>3 small potatoes, thinly sliced
>1 medium tomato, chopped

1. Brown onion in margarine. Add spices and brown lightly.
2. Stir in zucchini, potatoes, and tomato. Stir-fry about 15 minutes or until potatoes are cooked through.

Serve with rice for a true Indian curry flavor. We learned to love this during 11 years of living in India.

—Erma Sider, Fort Erie, Ontario

Soybean Burgers

>1 1/2 cups soybeans, cooked and ground
>1/2 cup bread crumbs
>1/2 tsp. soy sauce
>2 eggs
>1/2 tsp. salt
>1/4 tsp. onion salt
>dash of pepper

1. Mix all ingredients. Drop by spoonfuls into small amount of oil in medium hot skillet. Shape into patties with back of spoon. Cook slowly until patties are golden brown. May be served for supper between toasted buns, with catsup, pickles, lettuce, and alfalfa sprouts.

I make up large batches of soybeans, enlist "child labor" for turning the grinder, and then pack in 1½ cup portions in the freezer awaiting an "emergency."

—Elaine Good, Urbana, Illinois

Cool Rise Pizza Crust

Makes 2 12" pizza crusts

> 2¾–3½ *cups flour*
> 1 *pkg. dry yeast*
> 1½ *tsp. salt*
> 1 *Tbsp. butter, softened*
> 1 *cup hot water*
> 1 *egg*

1. In mixer bowl combine 1 cup flour, yeast, salt, and butter. Add hot water. Mix 2 minutes with electric mixer. Add egg and ½ cup more flour. Beat 1 more minute, then add remaining flour.
2. Knead.
3. Lightly grease bowl and dough. Let rise till doubled.
4. Grease pans generously. Pat out dough into pans.
5. Add pizza sauce of your choice and your favorite pizza toppings.
6. Bake at 400° for 20-25 minutes.

Note: If you like thicker pizza dough, let dough rise again after you put it on pizza pans.

—Edwina Stoltzfus, Lebanon, Pennsylvania

Chinese Dinner

Makes 8 servings

> 1¹/₂ *lbs. hamburger*
> 1–2 *cups onions, chopped*
> 2 *cups celery, chopped*
> 2 *cups zucchini, chopped*
> 2 *cups spinach, chopped*
> 2 *cups Swiss chard, chopped*
> 2 *cans cream of mushroom soup*
> 1 *can cream of chicken soup*
> 3 *Tbsp. soy sauce*
> *salt to taste*
> 1 *can Chinese vegetables (optional)*
> 4–6 *cups rice, cooked*
> *chow mein noodles*

1. Brown meat and onions. Add greens. Simmer till soft. Add soups, soy sauce, and salt.
2. Mix with Chinese vegetables and rice. Top with chow mein noodles.
3. Bake at 350°–375° for 30 minutes.

Note: Don't hesitate to substitute leftover gravy for some of the soup.

With new Asian friends in our church fellowship, we enjoy this at carry-in meals.

— **LaVerna Klippenstein, Winnipeg, Manitoba**

Ground Beef Oriental

Makes 6–8 servings

> 2 *onions, finely chopped*
> 1 *cup celery, sliced*
> 3 *tsp. butter or margarine*
> 1 *lb. ground beef*
> ¹/₂ *cup rice, uncooked*
> 1 *can cream of chicken soup*

1 can cream of mushroom soup
1½ cups water
¼ cup soy sauce
¼ tsp. pepper
salt to taste
1 can bean sprouts

1. Brown first 3 ingredients in skillet. Remove from skillet.
2. Brown beef and rice.
3. Combine next 6 ingredients in buttered 2-quart baking dish. Add browned ingredients and lightly stir in sprouts.
4. Bake covered at 350° for ½ hour. Uncover and continue baking for another 30 minutes.
5. Serve with crisp Chinese noodles.

—Lois Herr, Quarryville, Pennsylvania

Corned Beef Casserole

Makes 6 servings

12-oz. can corned beef, broken
1½ cups cheddar cheese, diced
10½-oz. can condensed cream of chicken soup
1¼ cups milk
½ cup onion, chopped
4 cups wide noodles, cooked and drained
¾ cup bread crumbs, buttered

1. Combine all ingredients except bread crumbs.
2. Pour into 2-quart greased baking dish. Top with bread crumbs.
3. Bake at 350° for 1 hour.

—Helen White, Edmonton, Alberta

Special Meat Balls

Makes 6 servings

Meat Balls

> 1½ lbs. ground beef
> ½ lb. ground pork
> 1 cup bread crumbs, firmly packed
> 1 cup applesauce
> 2 eggs, slightly beaten
> 1 onion, grated
> ½ tsp. mace
> ¼ tsp. allspice
> salt to taste

1. Mix all ingredients together lightly. Form into small balls.
2. Brown in hot fat and drop into hot gravy.

Gravy

> 3 Tbsp. butter
> ¼ cup flour
> 1 can condensed consommé
> 1 cup water
> 2 Tbsp. parsely, chopped

1. Combine all ingredients.
2. Simmer 30 minutes after meatballs have been added.
3. Serve with rice, corn and green salad.

—Hildegarde Baerg, Abbotsford, British Columbia

Taco Casserole

Makes 10–12 servings

> 2 lbs. hamburger
> 2 onions, chopped
> 1 tsp. Tabasco® sauce
> ½ tsp. garlic, minced
> 18 oz. tomato sauce
> 15-oz. can hot beans
> 12–14 oz. tortilla or nacho chips, broken
> ½ lb. cheddar cheese, shredded
> 1 cup sour cream
> ½ head lettuce, torn
> 1–2 cups tomatoes, chopped
> hot taco sauce

1. Brown hamburger and onions. Add next 4 ingredients.
2. Place broken chips on bottom of 9″ x 13″ baking dish. Top with hamburger mixture and cheese.
3. Bake at 300° for 30–45 minutes.
4. Top with sour cream. Bake a few more minutes.
5. Before serving top with lettuce, tomatoes, and taco sauce.

—Ruth Horst, Elkhart, Indiana

Chipped Beef Pot Pie

Makes 6 servings

1 cup onion, chopped
4 oz. dried beef, cut up
¹/₄ cup hot fat
2 Tbsp. flour
¹/₄–¹/₂ tsp. salt
¹/₄ tsp. pepper
2 cups carrots, sliced thin
2 cups potatoes, sliced thin
2 cups water
1 bouillon cube (beef)
pastry, to cover casserole (optional)

1. Sauté onions and beef in hot fat. Stir in flour and seasoning. Add remaining ingredients and bring to a boil. Cover and simmer 5 minutes.
2. Place in greased baking dish and top with pastry.
3. Bake at 425° for 25–30 minutes.

Note: In order to never have to make a pastry top especially for this recipe, I always save the leftovers whenever I bake pies. I either freeze the leftovers in the shape of a small circle, or else I cut every little scrap of leftovers into geometric shapes. When arranged on top of the casserole, it makes an attractive design.

— Ruth Naylor, Bluffton, Ohio

Sweet and Sour Beef

Makes 4 servings

2 cups beef, cubed and cooked
¹/₂ green pepper, cut in thin strips
¹/₂ onion, cut in thin strips
3 Tbsp. hot oil
pineapple juice, drained from 20-oz. can of pineapple chunks
²/₃ cup brown sugar, firmly packed
²/₃ cup water

¹/₃ cup ketchup
¹/₄ cup vinegar
2 Tbsp. cornstarch
20-oz. can pineapple chunks

1. Sauté beef, pepper, and onion in hot oil in skillet.
2. In saucepan combine pineapple juice with next 5 ingredients. Bring to a boil, stirring frequently until thickened.
3. Pour over beef mixture and stir in pineapple chunks. Simmer 10–15 minutes.
4. Serve over hot rice.

— *Rhoda Yoder, Jackson, Mississippi*

Dinner in a Pumpkin

Makes 4–6 servings

2 Tbsp. oil
2 lbs. ground beef
6 oz. ground ham
2 cloves garlic, minced
2¹/₂ Tbsp. onion, chopped
1 green pepper, chopped
1 tsp. vinegar
2 tsp. oregano, ground
2¹/₂ tsp. salt
¹/₃ cup stuffed green olives, chopped
1 can tomato sauce
3 eggs, beaten
1 tsp. pepper
³/₄ cup raisins (optional)
1 small pumpkin, seeds removed

1. In oil brown next 5 ingredients. Stir in remaining ingredients.
2. Pour into pumpkin and bake at 350° for 1 hour with lid on pumpkin.
3. Serve dinner from pumpkin, scooping out pumpkin meat also, if desired.

— *Marilyn Forbes, Lutherville, Maryland*

Sausage Rice Dinner

Makes 6–8 servings

> **1 lb. pork sausage**
> **³/₄ cup rice, uncooked**
> **2 cups tomatoes, cooked**
> **³/₄ cup onion, chopped fine**
> **1 tsp. salt**
> **1 tsp. chili powder**
> **2 cups hot water**
> **¹/₂ cup sharp cheese, grated**

1. Break sausage into pieces and cook slowly in large skillet for 12–15 minutes until evenly browned, pouring off fat as it accumulates. Remove sausage, leaving ¼ cup fat.
2. Add rice to fat in skillet. Cook and stir over low heat until rice is lightly browned. Stir in tomatoes, onion, salt, chili powder, hot water, and sausage. Pour into 2–2¹/₂ quart baking dish.
3. Bake uncovered at 350° for 40 minutes.
4. Sprinkle cheese on top and bake an additional 10 minutes.

—Becky Gehman, Bergton, Virginia

Sausage Fruit Bake

Makes 6 servings

> **1 lb. pork sausage**
> **1 lb. sweet potatoes, cooked and sliced**
> **1 lb. peaches, sliced**
> **3 tart cooking apples, cut in eighths**
> **2 Tbsp. butter, melted**
> **¹/₃ cup brown sugar, firmly packed**

1. Pan-fry sausage about 15 minutes. Drain off fat.
2. In 2-quart greased baking dish, alternate layers of sausage, sweet potatoes, and fruit. Pour butter over top and sprinkle with brown sugar.

3. Bake covered at 375° for 20 minutes. Uncover and bake 15 minutes longer or till apples are tender.

—Marilyn Zook, Hagerstown, Maryland

Puerto Rican Pork Chops

Makes 8 servings

> 8 pork chops, trimmed of excess fat
> pepper
> cumin
> oregano
> 2 garlic cloves, minced, or garlic powder
> salt
> flour
> 2 Tbsp. oil
> 1½ cups water
> 2 Tbsp. soy sauce

1. Lay chops side by side in large, shallow baking pan. Generously season both sides of chops with first 4 seasonings. Press seasonings into meat and sprinkle with salt. Lightly dust with flour.
2. Brown chops, a few at a time, in oil in heavy skillet till chops are a rich brown color. Transfer chops to baking pan.
3. Drain any excess oil from skillet and add water and soy sauce, stirring to gather up any bits left in the skillet.
4. Pour broth over chops in baking pan. Cover tightly with foil.
5. Bake at 350° for 1–1½ hours. Add more water from time to time if pan gets dry.

When our family has a get-together we always have a native feast. One of our favorite menus features Puerto Rican style pork chops, White Rice a la Caribe (see page 252), beans in sauce or Habichuelas (see page 249), a big green salad with avocados, tomatoes, and lettuce, dressed with a simple oil-vinegar dressing, crusty French Bread, and an un-typical, but tropical, dessert—Tropical Bananas (see page 270). Added bonus: leftover rice, beans, and pork, combined with chicken broth, makes a wonderful soup.

—Esther R. Graber, Aibonito, Puerto Rico

Hot Chicken Bake

Makes 6–8 servings

4 cups chicken or turkey, cooked and cut up
2 Tbsp. lemon juice
3/4 cup mayonnaise
2 cups celery, chopped
4 hard-boiled eggs, sliced
1 can cream of chicken soup
1 Tbsp. onion, chopped
2 Tbsp. pimento, chopped (optional)
1 1/2 cups cheddar cheese, grated
1 1/2 cups potato chips, crushed
2/3 cup almonds, slivered

1. Combine all ingredients except last 3. Place in rectangular baking dish. Top with cheese, chips, and almonds. Cover with plastic wrap.
2. Refrigerate overnight, or 12 hours.
3. Bake at 400° for 25–30 minutes.

—Hulda Schmidt, Glendive, Montana

Chicken Dinner

Makes 8 servings

1 can cream of mushroom soup
1/3 soup-can of milk
2 Tbsp. butter
1 1/4 cups cracker crumbs
2 cups rice, cooked
1 cup green peas
1 fryer, cooked, skinned and cut up
1/4 cup celery, chopped and cooked with chicken
1/4 cup onion, chopped and cooked with chicken
1/2 lb. mild cheese, grated
salt to taste
pepper to taste

Accent® (optional)

1. Combine and heat first 3 ingredients. Let cool.
2. Grease baking dish and cover bottom with half the cracker crumbs. Add in layers half of each of the remaining ingredients, beginning with rice and ending with the seasonings. Finally add the soup mixture. Then repeat the layers. Top with remaining half of the crumbs.
3. Bake at 350° for 50–60 minutes.

—Ida Knopp, Hayward, California

Hasen Pfeffer

Makes 4 servings

> **1 rabbit, cut in serving pieces**
> **vinegar**
> **water**
> **1 onion, sliced**
> **1 tsp. whole cloves**
> **3–4 bay leaves**
> **salt to taste**
> **pepper to taste**
> **butter**
> **1 cup sour cream**

1. Place rabbit in stone crock or stainless steel container and cover with equal parts of vinegar and water. Add onion and seasonings.
2. Soak in solution for 2 days.
3. Lift meat out of liquid and brown slowly in butter, turning often. Gradually add desired amount of pickling sauce and let simmer till meat is tender, about 45 minutes.
4. Before serving stir in sour cream.

—Irma Nyce, Doylestown, Pennsylvania

Scallops New England

Makes 6 servings

5 Tbsp. butter, melted
5 Tbsp. spinach, minced
2 Tbsp. onion, minced
3 Tbsp. lettuce, minced
2 Tbsp. celery, chopped fine
3 Tbsp. dry bread crumbs
1/4 tsp. herb (your choice)
dash pepper
1/2 tsp. salt
3 Tbsp. butter
36 sea scallops (2–2 1/2 lbs.)
paprika
garlic powder
dill weed

1. Combine first 9 ingredients together. Mix well.
2. Heat but do not let butter brown.
3. Place scallops in foil-lined broiler pan. Dot with 3 Tbsp. butter. Sprinkle with paprika, garlic powder, dill weed, and vegetable mixture.
4. Broil until lightly browned and heated through, about 10 minutes.

—Janet Swartzentruber, Worthington, Ohio

Easy Mincemeat

Makes filling for 2 pies

1 cup hamburger
1 cup water
1/2 tsp. salt
3 cups apples, chopped
3 cups raisins
1 cup brown sugar
1/3 cup vinegar, cider, or lemon juice
1 orange with peel, ground

1 tsp. cinnamon
1/2 tsp. cloves
1/2 tsp. nutmeg

Combine all ingredients. Cook until tender. No need to brown hamburger. Fills 2 pies.

—Hazel Miller, Hudson, Illinois

Grated Apple Pie

Makes 9" pie

> 2 eggs
> 1/3 cup sugar
> 2 Tbsp. cornstarch
> 3 Tbsp. butter
> 1/2 tsp. cinnamon
> 1/2 tsp. nutmeg
> 1/2 cup cream
> 5 large apples, juicy if possible
> 9" pie shell, unbaked (optional)

1. Blend first 7 ingredients in blender for a few seconds. Slice in apples and blend again. When apples are cut fine, pour into pie shell or pie plate without shell (pie holds shape without crust).
2. Bake at 400° for 30 minutes, or till ingredients are set.

—Mae Imhoff, Roanoke, Illinois

Canned Apple Filling

Makes 12 quarts

> **7 qts. fresh apples, peeled and sliced**
> **4¹/₂ cups sugar**
> **1 cup cornstarch**
> **2 tsp. cinnamon**
> **¹/₄ tsp. nutmeg**
> **1 tsp. salt**
> **10 cups water**
> **3 Tbsp. lemon juice**
> **¹/₂ cup butter**

1. Fill canning jars ³/₄ full of apples.
2. Boil sugar, cornstarch, cinnamon, nutmeg, salt, and water, till thickened.
3. Remove from heat. Add lemon juice and butter. Stir till well blended. Pour over apples into jars till jars are full.
4. Seal and process jars in boiling water for 25 minutes. Remove jars and make sure they are tightly sealed before storing.

Note: Filling jars too full may cause filling to bubble over, resulting in jars that are only half full and not sealed.

This is a ready to use product for pies, desserts or side dishes. Pour into an unbaked crust and bake at 375° for 1 hour. If soft apples are used, shorten baking time.

—Mrs. Harvey Harder, Mountain Lake, Minnesota

Apple Dumplings in a Casserole

Makes 6–8 servings

> **2 cups flour**
> **2½ tsp. baking powder**
> **½ tsp. salt**
> **⅔ cup shortening**
> **½ cup milk**
> **6-8 baking apples, peeled and cored**
> **1 cup brown sugar**
> **¾ cup sugar**
> **¼ cup margarine**
> **¼ tsp. cinnamon**

1. Combine flour, baking powder and salt. Cut in shortening. Add milk and mix to form a soft dough. Line a large, low casserole dish with ⅔ of the dough, reserving ⅓ for a top crust.
2. Schnitz or slice apples over the crust. Sprinkle sugars and cinnamon over the apples. Dot with margarine. Cover with remaining dough. Pinch edges to seal. Slit several times in the center for steam to escape. Bake at 375° for 40 minutes, or until apples are soft and crust is nicely browned. Serve warm with rich milk.

This was a Burck family favorite supper baked in a woodstove oven. With eight children Mother made two large dripping pans full and none was left over. We slept a little restlessly but, oh, the beautiful dreams!

—Evelyn Burck Fisher, Glendale, Arizona

Apple Cobbler

Makes 6–8 servings

> 5 cups tart apples, peeled and sliced
> 3/4 cup sugar
> 2 Tbsp. flour
> 1 Tbsp. lemon juice
> 1 tsp. vanilla
> 1/2 tsp. cinnamon
> 1/4 tsp. salt
> 2 Tbsp. butter
> 1/2 cup flour
> 1/2 cup sugar
> 1/2 tsp. baking powder
> 1/4 tsp. salt
> 2 Tbsp. margarine or butter, softened
> 1 egg, slightly beaten
> whipped cream or ice cream

1. Combine first 7 ingredients. Turn into 8″ square baking dish. Spread evenly and dot with 2 Tbsp. butter.
2. Combine next 6 ingredients and beat till smooth. Drop in 9 portions over filling in dish, spacing evenly. (Batter will spread during baking.)
3. Bake at 375° for 35–40 minutes, or till apples are tender and crust is golden.
4. Serve topped with cream or ice cream.

— Ida Knopp, Hayward, California

Raw Apple Cake

Makes 10–12 servings

> 3/4 cup butter or margarine
> 1 1/2 cups sugar
> 2 eggs, beaten
> 3/4 cup strong coffee
> 1 tsp. vanilla

2¼ cups flour, sifted
1½ tsp. baking soda
½ tsp. salt
3 cups apples, peeled and chopped

1. Cream butter and sugar. Beat in eggs. Add coffee and vanilla.
2. Mix dry ingredients. Add to mixture. Stir in apples. Pour into greased 9″ x 13″ x 2″ pan.

Topping

½ cup brown sugar
1 tsp. cinnamon
½ cup nuts, chopped

1. Mix together and spread over batter.
2. Bake at 350° for 45 minutes.

—Marilyn Forbes, Lutherville, Maryland

Zucchini Cake

Makes 1 long cake

2 cups grated zucchini
2 cups sugar
1 cup vegetable oil
3 eggs
2⅓ cups flour
¼ tsp. baking powder
1 tsp. salt
2 tsp. baking soda
3 tsp. vanilla
¼ cup dates, chopped
1 cup walnuts, broken (optional)

1. Combine zucchini, sugar, oil, and eggs. Beat well.
2. Sift flour, baking powder, salt, and soda together. Fold into zucchini mixture. Add vanilla, dates and nuts. Pour into greased 9″ x 13″ pan. Bake at 350° for 45 minutes. Frost with cream cheese frosting.

—Rita Baechler, Shakespeare, Ontario

Pumpkin Cake Roll

Makes 1 roll

3 eggs, beaten
1 cup sugar
²/₃ cup pumpkin
1 tsp. lemon juice
³/₄ cup flour
1 tsp. baking powder
¹/₂ tsp. salt
2 tsp. cinnamon
1 tsp. ginger
¹/₂ tsp. nutmeg
1 cup pecans, chopped

1. Combine first 4 ingredients.
2. Sift flour, baking powder, and spices. Add to egg mixture. Spread in greased and floured 15″ x 10″ x 1″ pan. Top with pecans.
3. Bake at 375° for 15 minutes.

Filling

¹/₂ cup confectioner's sugar
8 oz. cream cheese
4 Tbsp. butter

1. Mix sugar, cream cheese, and butter until smooth. Set aside.
2. Turn baked roll out on pastry board or linen towel, sprinkled with confectioner's sugar. Starting at narrow end, roll cake up with towel and cool.
3. Unroll pastry and spread with filling. Roll up and chill.

Note: Line the cake pan with waxed paper to be sure the cake comes away smoothly when turned onto the towel or pastry board. Let the cake cool a few minutes before rolling up in towel.

One year our son Justin brought home a tiny little sprouted pumpkin seed from kindergarten. The following fall we harvested 23 pumpkins from that vine, which had practically taken over our garden. Besides pumpkin pie and pumpkin custard we enjoyed this pumpkin cake roll, served usually for company dessert.

—Kathy Stoltzfus, Leola, Pennsylvania

Choco-Chip Pumpkin Cake

Makes 1 long cake

>   **2 cups sugar**
>   **4 eggs**
>   **2 cups cooked pumpkin**
>   **1 cup vegetable oil**
>   **2 cups flour**
>   **2 tsp. baking powder**
>   **1 tsp. baking soda**
>   **1/2 tsp. salt**
>   **1 1/2 tsp. cinnamon**
>   **1/2 tsp. cloves**
>   **1/4 tsp. allspice**
>   **1/4 tsp. ginger**
>   **1 cup bran cereal**
>   **1 cup chocolate chips**
>   **1 cup nuts, chopped**

1. Combine sugar and eggs. Beat well. Add pumpkin and oil and mix well.
2. Sift together flour, baking powder, baking soda, salt, and spices. Fold into pumpkin mixture. Stir in cereal, chips, and nuts. Pour into a greased and floured 9″ x 13″ pan. Bake at 350° for 40–50 minutes. Needs no frosting.

Note: Add 1/4 cup cocoa if more chocolate taste is desired.

—Jan Hertzler Buerge, Kansas City, Kansas

Scrumptious Coffee Cake

Makes 1 long cake

> ¹/₄ cup butter
> 1 cup sugar
> 2 eggs
> 2 cups flour
> 1 tsp. soda
> 1 tsp. baking powder
> ¹/₄ tsp. salt
> 1 cup sour cream
> 1 tsp. vanilla
> ¹/₄ cup nuts
> ¹/₄ cup brown sugar
> ¹/₄ cup sugar
> 1 tsp. cinnamon

1. Cream butter and sugar. Add eggs and beat well.
2. Sift flour, soda, baking powder, and salt together. Add alternately with sour cream. Add vanilla. Pour batter into a greased 9″ x 13″ pan.
3. Combine nuts, sugars, and cinnamon. Swirl on top of batter. Bake at 350° for 25–30 minutes.

Note: This coffee cake is served to guests at the Historic Wyck House in Germantown, Pennsylvania.

— *Marianna Stutzman, Philadelphia, Pennsylvania*

Shoo-Fly Cake

Makes 1 long cake

> 1 cup molasses (King Syrup® or dark Karo® syrup)
> 2¹/₄ cups boiling water
> 1 Tbsp. soda
> 4 cups flour
> ¹/₂ tsp. salt
> ³/₄ cup oil
> 2 cups brown sugar

1. Combine molasses, water, and soda. Set aside.
2. Combine remaining ingredients and mix until crumbly. Reserve 1½ cups crumbs for top of cake. Add molasses mixture to remaining crumbs. Mixture will be lumpy. Pour into a greased 9″ x 13″ pan. Sprinkle reserved crumbs evenly over top. Bake at 350° for 40–50 minutes.

—Edwina Stoltzfus, Lebanon, Pennsylvania

Crisp Ginger Cookies

1 cup butter or margarine
2 cups sugar
2 eggs
½ cup molasses or sorghum
4½ cups flour
1 tsp. baking soda
1 tsp. ginger
½ tsp. cinnamon
¼ tsp. nutmeg
½ tsp. salt
sugar

1. Cream butter and sugar. Add eggs and molasses. Mix thoroughly.
2. Sift dry ingredients. Add to creamed mixture.
3. Form dough into several rolls about 2½″ in diameter. (If dough is too soft, chill until it can be shaped). Chill rolls thoroughly or wrap and freeze.
4. Cut rolls in ¼″ thick slices. Dip cookie slices into sugar, and place sugar side up on greased cookie sheets.
5. Bake at 450° for 8–10 minutes. Do not bake too brown.

Note: The rolls of dough, wrapped for freezing, will keep for months in the freezer, making it possible to have freshly-baked cookies in a short time. The dough slices more easily when frozen.

—Barbara Hershberger, Glendale, Arizona

Raisin and Nut Cookies

Makes 8 dozen

> 3 eggs, beaten
> 1½ cups buttermilk
> 4 cups quick oatmeal
> 1½ cups raisins
> 1 cup nuts, chopped
> 1 cup light molasses or sorghum
> 1¼ cups granulated sugar
> 1¼ cups brown sugar
> 1¼ cups shortening
> 5½ cups flour
> 2 Tbsp. baking soda
> 2 Tbsp. baking powder
> ¼ tsp. nutmeg
> 1 Tbsp. cinnamon
> pinch salt
> 1 Tbsp. vanilla

1. Mix first 3 ingredients. Set aside.
2. Combine next 3 ingredients. Set aside.
3. Cream sugars and shortening. Add to egg mixture.
4. Sift remaining dry ingredients. Add to creamed mixture, along with raisin-nut mixture. Add vanilla. Let stand ½ hour in refrigerator.
5. Drop by teaspoons onto greased baking sheets.
6. Bake at 375° till golden brown, about 12–15 minutes.

— Pauline Yoder, Goshen, Indiana

Apple Brownies

Makes 30 brownies

> ½ cup butter
> 2 cups sugar
> 2 eggs
> 2 tsp. soda

2 Tbsp. hot water
2 cups flour
$\frac{1}{2}$ tsp. salt
2 tsp. cinnamon
1 cup nuts
6 medium apples, coarsely chopped

1. Cream butter, sugar, and eggs.
2. Add soda dissolved in hot water.
3. Sift dry ingredients together. Fold into creamed mixture.
   Stir in nuts and apples. Turn onto a large cookie sheet with $\frac{1}{2}''$ sides.
   Bake at 350° for 40–45 minutes. Cut into squares and serve.

Note: These are very moist. Keep in tight container.

—*Edwina Stoltzfus, Lebanon, Pennsylvania*

Date Pudding

Makes 10–12 servings

1 cup water, boiling
1 tsp. baking soda
1 cup dates, chopped
1 Tbsp. butter
pinch salt
1$\frac{1}{2}$ cups flour
1 cup sugar
1 egg
$\frac{1}{2}$ cup nuts, chopped
1 tsp. vanilla
whipped cream

1. Pour boiling water over baking soda, dates, and butter. Let stand till
   cool. Add remaining ingredients except whipped cream. Pour into 9″ x
   13″ baking pan.
2. Bake at 350° for 25 minutes.
3. Cut cake in squares and fold whipped cream into cake squares just before
   serving.

—*Janet Yoder, Phoenix, Arizona*
—*Arie Hochstetler, Goshen, Indiana*

Pumpkin Layer Dessert

Makes 12–15 servings

2 eggs, beaten
³/₄ cup sugar
8-oz. pkg. cream cheese, softened
1 graham cracker crust
¹/₂ cup sugar
¹/₂ tsp. salt
2 cups pumpkin, mashed
3 egg yolks
¹/₂ cup milk
1 Tbsp. cinnamon
1 pkg. plain gelatin
¹/₂ cup cold water
3 egg whites
¹/₄ cup sugar
whipped cream

1. Mix first 3 ingredients and pour into crust. Bake at 350° for 20 minutes.
2. Mix next 6 ingredients. Cook until thick. Remove from heat.
3. Dissolve gelatin in cold water. Add to thickened mixture. Cool thoroughly.
4. Beat egg whites and ¹/₄ cup sugar. Fold into cooled pumpkin mixture. Pour over crust and cheese layer. Chill several hours.
5. Cut into squares to serve and top with whipped cream.

—Gloria Lehman, Singers Glen, Virginia

Granola

Makes 3 quarts

6 cups oatmeal
¹/₂ cup nuts (walnuts, almonds, cashews)
1 cup soy flour
1 cup coconut
1 cup powdered milk

¹/₂ cup wheat germ
1 cup bran
¹/₄ cup brown sugar
1 cup honey
³/₄ cup oil

1. Mix first 8 ingredients in large bowl.
2. Combine honey and oil. Add to dry ingredients.
3. Place on cookie sheets or in 9″ x 13″ pan, and bake at 325° for 40 minutes, stirring every 10 minutes.
4. Cool on paper towels and store in jars.

—Judy Classen, Newton, Kansas

Tasty Grapes

2-2¹/₂ lbs. green or red seedless grapes
8-oz. container sour cream
¹/₄ cup brown sugar
¹/₄ tsp. cinnamon

1. Wash and stem grapes. Allow to dry.
2. Combine sour cream, sugar, and cinnamon. Mix until smooth. Pour over grapes. Chill well and serve. They will keep several days.

—Clara Burkholder, Smithville, Ohio

All Seasons

And so life and the seasons keep their eternal rhythms.

Marked by the shriveled seed that dies to live, the moon that falls from full circle to total darkness, the baby that passes into seasoned age, so moves the earth in its path to and from the sun. And we are sustained by a host of fruits and lively memories from many times and places.

Bring on the Whole Wheat Apple-Honey Bread. Let's try Arroz Con Pollo. We have Crepes de la Robertsau!

While the earth remains, seedtime and harvest, cold and heat, summer and winter, and day and night shall not cease.

—Genesis 8:22

Whole Wheat Apple-Honey Bread

Makes 2 loaves

> **2 cups warm water**
> **2 Tbsp. dry yeast**
> **¼ cup oil**
> **½ cup apple butter or applesauce**
> **½ cup honey**
> **4 cups whole wheat flour**
> **3–4 cups white flour**
> **2 tsp. cinnamon, if using applesauce (optional)**

1. Pour the warm water into a large bowl. Add the yeast and let dissolve. Then add the oil, honey, apple butter or applesauce. Blend together with wire whisk or wooden spoon; then stir in the whole wheat flour. Next add the white flour, using only enough to make the dough stiff enough to knead. Turn out on a slightly floured board to knead, or knead it in the bowl for 2–3 minutes.
2. Cover and set aside in a warm place for about 45–60 minutes, or until it doubles. Punch down, shape into loaves and place into well-greased pans. Let rise about 40–50 minutes.
3. Place in preheated 375° oven for 30–35 minutes. Cool on racks.

Note: Don't let the dough over-rise the second time. If it does, punch it down, reshape, and let it rise again, shortening the time by 5–10 minutes.

—Lois Friesen, Towanda, Kansas

Sourdough English Muffins

Makes 8–10 muffins

> *¹/₂ cup sourdough starter*
> *1 cup milk*
> *1¹/₄ cups whole wheat flour*
> *1¹/₄ cups unbleached flour*
> *¹/₂ tsp. salt*
> *¹/₂ tsp. baking soda*
> *1 Tbsp. honey*

1. Combine sourdough starter, milk, 1 cup whole wheat flour, and 1 cup unbleached flour in bowl. Cover and let stand at room temperature 8–12 hours. Mix into it the remaining flour, salt, baking soda, and honey.
2. Place the sticky dough on cornmeal coated board. Sprinkle with additional cornmeal. Roll ³/₄" thick. Cut.
3. Fry 10 minutes per side in lightly greased skillet at 275°. Serve warm with butter and a drizzle of honey.

— *Glenda Knepp, Turner, Michigan*

Pumpkin Nut Bread

Makes 2 Loaves

> *²/₃ cup oil*
> *2 cups honey*
> *4 eggs*
> *2 cups cooked pumpkin*
> *¹/₄ cup water*
> *3¹/₃ cups whole wheat flour*
> *¹/₂ tsp. baking powder*
> *2 tsp. baking soda*
> *1 tsp. salt*
> *1 tsp. cinnamon*
> *¹/₂ tsp. cloves*
> *²/₃ cup chopped nuts*
> *²/₃ cup raisins*

1. Mix together oil, honey, eggs, pumpkin and water. Add remaining ingredients except nuts and raisins. Stir in nuts and raisins.
2. Bake at 350° for 50–60 minutes in two greased 9″ bread pans. Let cool before slicing.

—Glenda Knepp, Turner, Michigan

Whole Grain Muffins

Makes 12 muffins

> **2 cups whole wheat flour**
> **1 cup bran**
> **¼ cup dry milk powder**
> **1 Tbsp. baking powder**
> **¼ tsp. salt**
> **1 cup milk**
> **¼ cup oil**
> **¼ cup honey**

1. Combine flour, bran, milk powder, baking powder, and salt in bowl. Add milk, oil, and honey.
2. Bake 12–14 minutes at 375° in 12 greased muffin tins.

—Glenda Knepp, Turner, Michigan

Jamuffins

Makes 12–14 muffins

2 cups whole wheat flour, or
  1 cup whole wheat flour plus 1 cup unbleached flour
1 Tbsp. baking powder
¹/₂ tsp. baking soda
¹/₄ cup oil
¹/₄ cup honey
¹/₄ cup milk
1 cup plain yogurt
1 egg
¹/₂ tsp. vanilla
12 rounded teaspoons jam or apple butter

1. Mix together the flour, baking powder, and baking soda. Add remaining ingredients except jam and spoon half of the batter into greased muffin pans.
2. Place jam or apple butter over batter in each muffin cup. Top with remaining batter.
3. Bake at 400° for 15–20 minutes. Let stand 5 minutes before removing from pans.

—*Glenda Knepp, Turner, Michigan*

Oatmeal Pancakes

Makes 12 pancakes

> **1¹/₂ cups rolled oats**
> **1 cup yogurt or 1 cup sour milk**
> **1 cup milk**
> **²/₃ cup whole wheat flour**
> **1 tsp. soda**
> **¹/₂ tsp. salt**
> **2 eggs**

1. Mix oats, yogurt and milk. Beat in remaining ingredients.
2. Bake on hot, lightly greased skillet.

Note: This pancake batter can be prepared ahead of time and refrigerated up to 8 hours, until you're ready to bake.

—Glenda Knepp, Turner, Michigan

Whole Wheat Pancakes

Makes 12 thick pancakes

> **1 cup yogurt or 1 cup sour milk**
> **1 cup milk**
> **¹/₄ cup oil**
> **2 eggs**
> **2 cups whole wheat flour**
> **2 tsp. baking powder**
> **1 tsp. soda**
> **¹/₂ tsp. salt**

1. Combine yogurt, milk, and oil. Add flour, baking powder, soda, and salt, mixing gently.
2. Bake as usual on hot, lightly greased skillet.

—Glenda Knepp, Turner, Michigan

Cheese Pancakes Plus

Makes 3 servings

>3 eggs, well beaten
>1 cup cottage cheese, sieved
>2 Tbsp. vegetable oil
>¼ cup flour, sifted
>¼ tsp. salt

1. Combine eggs, cheese, and oil.
2. Stir in dry ingredients only until blended.
3. Bake on griddle. Spread with jelly or jam and roll up. Sprinkle with confectioner's sugar.

This works as well for supper as for breakfast!

—Edna Brunk, Upper Marlboro, Maryland

Fruit Topping for Pancakes

>1 cup water
>2 Tbsp. cornstarch
>⅓ cup honey
>4 cups unsweetened blueberries or other fruit

Combine and bring to a boil the water, cornstarch, and honey. Add fruit. Bring to boil again and serve.

—Glenda Knepp, Turner, Michigan

Baked Hotcakes and Sausage

Makes 4 servings

¹/₂ lb. sausage, browned
2 Tbsp. butter or margarine, melted
²/₃ cup milk
1 egg beaten
1 cup flour
2 Tbsp. sugar
2 tsp. baking powder
¹/₄ tsp. salt
¹/₄ tsp. cinnamon
¹/₄ tsp. nutmeg
¹/₂ cup apples, finely chopped

1. Mix liquid ingredients together. Set aside.
2. Stir dry ingredients together. Mix liquid into dry ingredients.
3. Fold in apples.
4. Pour into a greased 11″ x 7″ baking dish and top with sausage.
5. Bake at 450° for 15 minutes. Serve warm with butter and maple syrup.

Variation:
   Substitute browned bacon for sausage.

I like to serve this with fresh fruit for breakfast or brunch to house guests at any time of the year.

—Edna Brunk, Upper Marlboro, Maryland

Pflinzen (Russian Pancakes)

Makes 4 servings

> 2 *eggs*
> 2 *cups milk*
> 2 *cups flour*
> *dash of salt*

1. Heat a lightly greased skillet until drops of water dance. While tilting skillet in a circular motion, pour in just enough batter to coat the bottom. Flip over in a minute or two and brown second side lightly. Repeat, adding a half teaspoon oil to skillet between each pancake.
2. Roll one or two on a fork and put on your plate. Serve with any nonsugary filling such as peanut butter and honey, fruit sauces or cottage cheese or yogurt with fruit.

—Doris Longacre

Russian Mennonite Porzelky

> 1 *pkg. yeast*
> $^1/_2$ *cup warm water*
> 1 *tsp. sugar*
> 2 *cups milk, scalded and cooled to lukewarm*
> $^1/_4$ *cup butter or margarine*
> 3 *eggs*
> $^1/_4$ *cup sugar*
> 1 *tsp. salt*
> 2 *cups raisins*
> 4–5 *cups flour*
> *granulated or powdered sugar*

1. Mix yeast, water, and sugar together and let stand 5 minutes. Combine remaining ingredients in large mixing bowl. Use enough flour so that dough is thick but still soft. Beat very well, until dough is glossy and smooth. Cover bowl and allow to rise until dough is doubled.
2. With a teaspoon, cut off pieces of dough and drop into hot fat. Deep-fry until golden brown. Dip spoon into hot fat occasionally to keep dough

from sticking. Drain on absorbent paper, then sprinkle with granulated or powdered sugar.

—Doris Longacre

Parisian Vegetable Soup

Makes 12 servings

> 2¹/₂ cups mixed vegetables — broccoli, cauliflower and carrots
> 2 cups water
> ¹/₂ cup onion
> ¹/₂ cup celery
> 2 sticks margarine
> 1 cup flour
> 6 cups milk
> 1 cup ham, chopped
> 4 bouillon cubes (chicken)
> 1 tsp. pepper
> salt to taste

1. Cook vegetables in water until tender. Do not drain.
2. Sauté the onions and celery in margarine. When tender blend in flour. Stir mixture and add milk. Stir until smooth and thick.
3. Add remaining ingredients along with cooked vegetables in juice. Add salt to taste and simmer, stirring frequently.

—Marge Grieser, Toledo, Ohio

Chili

Makes 6 pints

Canned Chili Sauce

>1¹/₂ *cups onions, chopped*
>1 *cup green peppers, chopped*
>1¹/₂ *cups celery, chopped*
>6 *qts. tomatoes, chopped*
>¹/₃ *cup white vinegar*
>¹/₃ *cup sugar*
>3 *tsp. salt*
>1 *Tbsp. whole allspice*
>1 *Tbsp. whole cloves*
>2" *piece cinnamon stick*
>2 *bay leaves*
>1 *tsp. ginger*
>1 *tsp.–1 Tbsp. chili powder*

1. Combine chopped vegetables with vinegar, sugar, and salt. Add spices tied loosely in cheesecloth bag and cook slowly in huge kettle (about 1¹/₂ hours).
2. Remove spice bag. Seal while still hot. Makes 6 pints sauce. Can also be cooled and stored in refrigerator.

Chili Soup

Makes 12 servings

>1¹/₂–2 *lbs. hamburger*
>1 *or 2 cans kidney beans*
>1 *can tomato soup*
>2 *cups water*
>1 *pint chili sauce (above recipe)*

1. Brown hamburger and drain grease. Add remaining ingredients.
2. Heat together and simmer slowly for 20 minutes. Serve with crackers.

—*Vivian Gering, Freeman, South Dakota*

Pa. Dutch Chicken Corn Soup

Makes 6–8 servings

> **1 large chicken or stewing hen**
> **4 qts. water**
> **1 onion, chopped**
> **2–3 tsp. salt**
> **pepper**
> **pinch of basil**
> **2 cups corn**
> **1/2 cup celery, finely chopped with leaves**
> **1–2 cups fine noodles**
> **2 hard-cooked eggs, chopped**
> **parsley**

1. Cook the chicken, water, onion, salt, pepper, and basil slowly until chicken is tender. Remove chicken and strain broth. Skim excess fat from broth. Take meat from bones, chop, and return to broth.
2. Reheat soup and add corn, celery, and noodles. Simmer until noodles are tender. Check seasoning. Just before serving add eggs and parsley.

—Doris Longacre

Apple-Grapefruit Salad

Makes 8 servings

> **2 cups grapefruit sections**
> **6-oz. pkg. lime gelatin**
> **2 cups boiling water**
> **1 1/2 cups apples, unpared and diced**
> **1/2 cups nuts, chopped**

1. Drain grapefruit, reserving juice.
2. Dissolve gelatin in boiling water. Add grapefruit juice, plus enough cold water to make 1 cup. Chill until slightly thickened.
3. Add apple, grapefruit, and chopped nuts. Pour into 1-qt. mold. Chill until set.

—Jean Shenk, Mt. Joy, Pennsylvania

Cabbage Salad

Makes 10–12 servings

> **large head of cabbage**
> **medium-sized onion**
> **1 cup sugar**

1. Shred cabbage and onion. Mix together.
2. Stir in sugar and let stand while making Dressing.

Dressing

> **2 Tbsp. sugar**
> **1 tsp. salt**
> **1 tsp. dry mustard or mustard seed**
> **1 tsp. celery salt or celery seed**
> **³/₄ cup vinegar**
> **¹/₂ cup salad oil**

1. Mix all ingredients together well. Bring to boil. Pour over cabbage and let stand until cool. Stir.
2. Place in refrigerator to chill. Let stand 24 hours before serving. (Keeps in refrigerator for one week.)

—Anna Ruth Beck, Halstead, Kansas

Carrot-Pineapple-Wheat Salad

Makes 8–10 servings

> *2¹/₂ cups carrots, shredded*
> *2 cups whole wheat kernels, cooked*
> *8-oz. can crushed, unsweetened pineapple, drained*
> *¹/₂ cup salad dressing or mayonnaise*

Combine ingredients and chill for several hours before serving.

Note: I usually cook the whole wheat kernels in a slow cooker—1 cup wheat kernels to 2 cups water—and freeze them in 1-cup plastic bags. That saves a lot of time when I want to use the kernels in salads and casseroles.

—Anna Ruth Beck, Halstead, Kansas

Cottage Cheese Salad

Makes 6 servings

> *6-oz. pkg. lemon or lime gelatin*
> *20-oz. can crushed pineapple*
> *1 lb. cottage cheese*
> *1 cup milk*
> *1 cup salad dressing or mayonnaise*

1. Drain pineapple. Heat juice and pour over gelatin, stirring until dissolved.
2. In another bowl, whip mayonnaise or salad dressing with whisk. Gradually add milk and stir until smooth. Add cottage cheese and pineapple and mix well. Add gelatin mixture and blend well.
3. Pour into mold which has been liberally rubbed with mayonnaise or salad dressing. Chill until set.

—Betty Pellman, Millersville, Pennsylvania

Vietnamese Chicken Salad

Serves about 6

> ¼ *cup salad oil*
> 2 *Tbsp. wine vinegar (or cider vinegar)*
> 2 *Tbsp. soy sauce*
> 2 *cloves garlic, finely chopped or pressed*
> 1 *tsp. sugar*
> ½ *tsp. salt*
> *few dashes freshly ground pepper*
> 4 *cups thinly sliced cabbage*
> 1 *carrot, finely grated*
> 2 *cups fresh bean sprouts or 1 cup canned sprouts, drained*
> 1–2 *cups cooked diced chicken*
> 3–4 *green onions with tops, sliced*
> ⅓ *cup roasted peanuts, chopped*

1. Combine in small bowl and let flavors blend at least 20 minutes: salad oil, vinegar, soy sauce, garlic, sugar, salt and pepper.
2. Mix together in large bowl remaining ingredients (except peanuts). If preparing in advance, chill vegetable mixture in covered bowl.
3. Just before serving, toss vegetable mixture with dressing and about half the peanuts.
4. Arrange salad on serving plate and sprinkle remaining peanuts on top.
Note: Cold cooked shrimp or cooked, thinly sliced pork can be substituted for chicken.

—*Doris Longacre*

Habichuelas — Beans in Sauce

Makes 8 servings

> 1 lb. dried red small beans
> ³/₄ lb. pumpkin or squash
> 2 qts. water

Wash beans and soak overnight in water to cover generously. In the morning, drain the beans and add water and the pumpkin or squash, cut in large cubes. Cook until the beans are almost tender.

Sauce (Sofrito)

> 1 Tbsp. oil
> ¹/₂–1 cup smoked ham, cubed
> 1 large onion, chopped
> 1 green pepper, chopped
> 2 cloves garlic, peeled and minced
> 2 sweet chili peppers, chopped
> ¹/₂ tsp. oregano leaves
> 2 tsp. salt
> 8-oz. can tomato sauce
> ¹/₄ cup (more or less to taste) fresh, chopped
>   coriander leaves

1. Sauté the ham in the oil. Add onions, green pepper, garlic and chili peppers, stirring over moderate heat until onion is transparent (about 10 minutes). Add oregano, salt, tomato sauce and fresh coriander.
2. When beans are almost tender, mash some of the chunks of pumpkin or squash inside the kettle and add the tomato sauce mixture to the pot. Continue to cook uncovered for about 1 hour, or until sauce thickens slightly and beans are soft. Adjust for salt.

—Esther R. Graber, Aibonito, Puerto Rico

Scalloped Broccoli and Corn

Makes 6 servings

> 1½ **cups broccoli, chopped**
> 2 **cups corn, creamed**
> 2 **eggs, slightly beaten**
> ½ **cup cultured sour cream**
> 1 **tsp. flour**
> ½ **tsp. seasoned salt**
> 1 **cup buttered bread cubes or french-fried onions**

1. Layer broccoli on bottom of greased 10″ x 6″ casserole.
2. In bowl mix together rest of ingredients, except bread or onion topping.
3. Layer half of mixture over broccoli. Cover with half of bread or onion topping.
4. Pour rest of mixture over.
5. Bake uncovered at 350° for 30–35 minutes.
6. Top with rest of bread cubes or onions and bake an additional 5 minutes.
Note: If doubling this recipe, bake in a 9″ x 13″ baking dish.

This casserole works well with fresh vegetables or with frozen ones when broccoli and corn are out of season.

—Marilyn Forbes, Lutherville, Maryland

Onion Casserole

Makes 6 servings

> 4 **cups onions, sliced**
> ½ **stick butter or margarine**
> ½ **cup almonds, slivered**
> 1 **can cream of mushroom soup**
> ½ **cup seasoned filling crumbs**

1. Parboil onions. Add melted butter and mushroom soup.
2. Pour into buttered casserole, top with filling and almonds. Bake at 350° for 30–40 minutes.

—Betty Pellman, Millersville, Pennsylvania

Argentina Noquis

Makes 6–8 servings

> **4 medium-sized potatoes**
> **salt**
> **2 cups flour**
> **tomato sauce**
> **parmesan cheese, grated**

1. Peel potatoes and cook until tender. Drain potatoes, reserving water. Mash the potatoes while hot, adding salt and just enough potato water to make them smooth but slightly thicker than for mashed potatoes. Add flour, enough so that the dough is slightly soft but can be handled.
2. On a floured board, roll dough into long ropes about ½″ thick. Cut into 1″ lengths. Drop noquis into a large kettle of simmering salted water. Each piece of dough may be rubbed across the tines of a fork to give it an attractive ribbed appearance, like shell macaroni. Simmer noquis about 10 minutes, then lift out with slotted spoon and drain.
3. Arrange on a platter and add hot tomato sauce and cheese.

—Doris Longacre

Country Carrots

> **whole large carrots**
> **2 Tbsp. margarine or butter**
> **brown sugar**
> **salt**
> **pepper**
> **parsley**

1. Scrub (do not peel) carrots. Cook gently until tender in just enough water to cover, allowing up to 40 minutes.
2. Drain carrots and slice lengthwise (½″ thick) onto serving plate.
3. Drizzle with margarine and sprinkle with a little brown sugar, salt, and pepper. Garnish with parsley and serve hot.

—Doris Longacre

Sour Cream Potatoes

Makes 10–12 servings

> 5 lbs. potatoes (about 9 large), peeled
> 2 3-oz. pkgs. cream cheese
> 1 cup cultured sour cream
> 2 tsp. onion salt
> 1 tsp. salt
> 1/4 tsp. pepper
> 2 Tbsp. butter or margarine, softened
> 3/4 cup milk

1. Cook potatoes until tender, then drain. Mash until smooth.
2. Add remaining ingredients, except milk, and beat until light and fluffy.
3. Add milk and beat until smooth.
4. Place in buttered casserole dish and dot with additional butter or margarine.
5. Cover and refrigerate casserole until ready to bake. When ready, bake covered at 350° for 45–60 minutes or until heated through.

Note: This casserole may be refrigerated up to 5 or more days before baking. It also freezes well.

—**Charlotte Croyle, Archbold, Ohio**

White Rice a la Caribe

Makes 8 servings

> 4 1/2 cups water
> 3 tsp. salt
> 6 Tbsp. vegetable oil
> 3 cups rice

1. Bring water, salt and oil to a boil in a large, heavy kettle with a tight-fitting lid.
2. Meanwhile, wash and drain the rice at least three times. Drain thoroughly in a sieve before adding to the boiling water.

3. Cook uncovered over moderate heat without stirring until water is absorbed and rice appears dry. With a fork, lift the rice from the bottom to top. Cover tightly, turn heat to low and cook for another 20 minutes. Halfway during this cooking period, again turn the rice with a fork.

—Esther R. Graber, Aibonito, Puerto Rico

Cheesy Scrambled Eggs

Makes 4–6 servings

> *2 Tbsp. onion, chopped*
> *1 Tbsp. oil*
> *5 eggs*
> *1/3 cup milk*
> *1/8 tsp. pepper*
> *1/4 tsp. salt*
> *1/3 cup cheese, grated*

1. Sauté chopped onion and oil together. Add eggs, milk, pepper, and salt and mix together. Add cheese.
2. Cook over medium heat; turn gently as mixture cooks.

—Glenda Knepp, Turner, Michigan

Crepes de la Robertsau

Makes 12 crepes

Crepe Batter

> **1 cup all-purpose flour**
> **¼ tsp. baking powder**
> **¼ tsp. salt**
> **1¼ cups milk**
> **1 egg**
> **1 Tbsp. butter or margarine, melted**

1. Mix flour, baking powder, and salt. Stir in remaining ingredients. Beat with hand beater until smooth.
2. Lightly butter small skillet (8″ or 9″) and heat until bubbly. For each crepe pour scant ¼ cup of batter into skillet and rotate skillet immediately so batter covers the pan. Cook until light brown. Turn with wide spatula and cook other side until light brown. Fill each crepe with desired filling, or stack with waxed paper between each crepe until ready to use.

Crepe au Fromage (Cheese)

> **2 Tbsp. butter**
> **2 Tbsp. flour**
> **¼ tsp. salt**
> **⅛ tsp. pepper**
> **1 cup milk**
> **1½ cups cheddar or Swiss cheese, shredded**
> **1 cup smooth cottage cheese** (fromage blanc)
> **parmesan cheese**
> **paprika**
> **parsley flakes**

1. Make white sauce by mixing butter, flour, salt, pepper, and milk together. Stir in cheddar or Swiss cheese and stir until melted. Add *fromage blanc* (smooth cottage cheese).
2. Put a tablespoon of cheese sauce on crepe and roll up. Place in baking casserole. Top with parmesan cheese and paprika and parsley flakes.
3. Bake at 350° for 20 minutes.

Crepe de la Mer (Shrimp)

> 1 can cream of mushroom or celery soup
> 1/2 can milk (or a bit less)
> 6- or 8-oz. can cooked shrimp
> 1/2 cup mushrooms, sliced
> 1/4–1/2 tsp. curry powder
> 2 cups tomato sauce
> parmesan cheese, grated

1. Stir the soup and the milk together. Stir in shrimp and heat. Add mushrooms and season with curry powder.
2. Put a spoonful on each crepe and roll up. Place in baking dish. Top with tomato sauce and parmesan cheese.
3. Bake at 350° for 20 minutes.

Crepe du Monde (Chicken)

> 4 Tbsp. butter
> 2 Tbsp. scallions, finely chopped
> 4 Tbsp. flour
> 1 1/4 cups milk or light cream
> 3/4 cup chicken broth
> 2 cups chicken, chopped
> mushrooms, sautéed
> parsley

1. Melt butter in saucepan. Add scallions and cook for 2 minutes. Add flour and stir to blend. Slowly add 1 cup of the milk. Add broth and seasonings and cook slowly until thick. Mix one-half of the white sauce with the chicken and add salt.
2. Fill each crepe with 2 or 3 Tbsp. of filling. Roll and place in dish. To the rest of the sauce add other 1/4 cup milk and sautéed mushrooms. Pour over the crepes and sprinkle with parsley.
3. Bake at 350° for 20–25 minutes.

> —Paul Kraybill, Allée de la Robertsau, Strasbourg, France

Verenicke

Makes 4–6 servings

> **3 egg whites, whipped**
> **¹/₂ cup milk**
> **2 cups flour**
> **1 tsp. salt**

Mix above ingredients to make dough, using more or less flour to be able to roll out fairly thin.

Filling

> **³/₄–1 pt. dry cottage cheese**
> **3 egg yolks**

1. Put 1 heaping teaspoon of cheese mixture on rolled out dough. Fold over and cut with cookie cutter. Pinch edges together.
2. Drop in boiling salted water; bring to a boil. Drain in colander.

Sauce

Fry sausage or slices of ham. Use fat to fry 1 medium onion till golden. Add 1 cup sour cream and heat. Individuals may spoon sauce over verenicke.

This is no doubt a dish which Mennonites learned about from their neighbors in Russia. Perhaps that explains why there's not even a right way, certainly not a consistent way, to spell verenicke.

I've always believed that no one would like this dish unless he/she grew up with it. But our son-in-law from Connecticut, who never saw a Mennonite until he met our daughter, loves the dish!

—Marie Wiens, Hillsboro, Kansas

Albondigas

Makes 4–6 servings

> 1 lb. lean ground beef
> 1 onion, chopped
> 1 egg
> ¼ tsp. oregano
> ½ tsp. cumin powder
> 1 clove garlic, minced
> ½ tsp. salt
> ¼ tsp. pepper
> 4 Tbsp. white rice, uncooked
> ⅓ cup bread crumbs
> 1 cup chicken broth or bouillon
> 2 cups tomato sauce or juice

1. Combine all ingredients except chicken broth and tomato sauce in large bowl. Mix well. Shape in small balls the size of a walnut and set aside.
2. Combine chicken broth and tomato sauce in large saucepan. Heat the sauce to boiling and drop in meatballs. When mixture boils again, reduce heat, cover pan, and simmer one hour.

—Doris Longacre

East African Meat Stew with Pancakes

1 lb. cubed beef or mutton
1 tsp. salt
¼ tsp. pepper
1 onion, chopped
1 green pepper, chopped
2 large potatoes, diced
1 cup yellow squash or sweet potato, diced
2–3 carrots, sliced
2 cups tomatoes, chopped
1 tsp. ground cardamom
1 tsp. chili powder
½ tsp. garlic salt
½ tsp. paprika
¼ tsp. curry powder

1. Brown beef, salt, and pepper in deep skillet or Dutch oven. Add and sauté onion and pepper.
2. Add 2 cups water. Cook slowly for an hour, or until meat is tender.
3. Add potatoes, squash, carrots, and tomatoes. Bring to boil and add spice mixture (cardamom, chili powder, garlic salt, paprika, and curry powder). Cook gently for another hour. Sauce may be thickened slightly with flour or cornstarch, if desired.

Pancakes (Anjero)

1½ cups flour
½ cup white cornmeal
1 tsp. salt
2 eggs
2 cups buttermilk
½ cup water

1. Combine flour, white cornmeal, and salt in a mixing bowl. Make a well in the mixture and add eggs, buttermilk, and water. Beat until smooth. Batter will be thin.
2. Heat iron skillet. Wipe with oil. With ladle, pour batter onto griddle, spreading thinly to make large round pancake. Cover pancake with large lid and cook until golden underneath and firm on top. Repeat, wiping griddle with oil before frying each pancake.

3. To eat, tear off pieces of pancake and use to scoop up the stew, or eat with stew over pancakes, using forks.

—*Doris Longacre*

American Chop Suey

Makes 10-12 servings

> **1 lb. ground beef**
> **2 small onions, chopped**
> **1½ cups celery, chopped**
> **1 can cream of mushroom soup**
> **2 soup cans of water**
> **¼ cup soy sauce**
> **¾ cup raw rice**

1. Brown meat. Then stir in onion, celery, soup, water, and sauce. Mix well.
2. Spread uncooked rice in bottom of greased 9″x13″ baking pan. Pour meat and vegetable mixture over rice.
3. Bake covered at 350° for 1 hour.

—*June Marie Weaver, Harrisonburg, Virginia*

Broccoli with Beef

Serves 4–5

> ¹/₂ lb. lean beef, sliced into thin bite-size strips
> ¹/₂ tsp. sugar
> 3 Tbsp. soy sauce
> 2 cloves garlic, minced
> 1 onion, chopped
> ³/₄ cup beef bouillon
> 1 Tbsp. cornstarch
> 1 bunch broccoli
> 3 Tbsp. cooking oil

1. Marinate beef, sugar, 1 Tbsp. soy sauce, garlic, and onion together about 20 minutes.
2. Stir together and set aside the beef bouillon, 2 Tbsp. soy sauce, and cornstarch.
3. Slice broccoli stems into 2″ lengths the width of carrot sticks, heads into 2″ florets.
4. Heat cooking oil in a skillet. Add broccoli and stir-fry over high heat 3-4 minutes, sprinkling with salt. Transfer broccoli to serving plate. Add 1 Tbsp. oil to skillet and stir-fry beef mixture just until it loses its red color. Add broccoli plus sauce mixture to beef; cook and stir until sauce thickens. Serve immediately with hot rice.

—Doris Longacre

Missouri Baked Ham

Makes 6 servings

> 3 slices ham, ³/₄″ thick
> ²/₃ cup dry bread crumbs or crushed cracker crumbs
> 2 Tbsp. brown sugar
> 2 tsp. dry mustard
> 2 egg yolks, beaten
> 2 tsp. Worcestershire® sauce
> milk

1. Place ham slices into a greased 9"x13" baking pan.
2. Mix crumbs, sugar, mustard, egg yolks, and sauce together into a paste.
3. Pour milk over ham slices to half cover the meat.
4. Spread paste over meat slices.
5. Bake uncovered at 325° for 45 minutes.

Ferne Savanick, Scottdale, Pennsylvania

Chicken with Rice

Makes 6–8 servings

> *2¹/₂–3 lbs. chicken, cut up*
> *1¹/₂ cups brown rice*
> *1 cup onions, chopped*
> *2 cloves garlic, minced*
> *3 cups water*
> *1 cup canned tomatoes, or equivalent*
> *1 Tbsp. bouillon or miso (optional)*
> *1 tsp. salt.*
> *¹/₄ tsp. pepper*
> *1–2 cups peas, frozen*

1. Brown chicken. Remove from skillet. In the drippings, sauté rice, onions, and garlic.
2. Add remaining ingredients and bring to a boil, stirring well.
3. Arrange chicken atop rice. Cover and simmer about 45–50 minutes. Stir in peas the last five minutes.

Note: One piece of chicken per diner still flavors the chicken rice combination very well.

—Glenda Knepp, Turner, Michigan

Pecan Buttermilk Chicken

Makes 8 servings

> **8–10 serving pieces of chicken**
> **¹/₂ cup butter or margarine**
> **1 egg, beaten**
> **1 cup buttermilk**
> **1 cup flour**
> **1 cup pecans, ground**
> **1 scant Tbsp. paprika**
> **1 Tbsp. salt**
> **¹/₈ tsp. pepper**
> **¹/₄ cup sesame seeds**
> **¹/₄ cup pecan halves**

1. Melt butter in 13″ x 9″ x 2″ baking pan.
2. Stir buttermilk into egg in shallow bowl.
3. Mix flour, ground pecans, paprika, salt, pepper, and sesame seeds together in another shallow bowl.
4. Dip chicken in buttermilk-egg mixture, then dip into flour mixture.
5. Put skin-side down in melted butter in baking pan to coat. Then turn chicken skin-side up for baking.
6. Drop pecan halves over and around chicken, then bake at 350° for 1³/₄ hours.

This is a rich, flavorful way to make chicken a party!

—Phyllis Pellman Good, Lancaster, Pennsylvania

Peanut Butter Cream Pie

Makes 1 pie

> **2 Tbsp. flour**
> **2 Tbsp. cornstarch**
> **¹/₂ tsp. salt**
> **²/₃ cup sugar**
> **2 cups milk**

1 tsp. vanilla
1 Tbsp. butter
1/2 cup peanut butter
3 eggs, separated
baked pie shell

1. Blend flour, cornstarch, salt, and sugar in saucepan. Add milk.
2. Cook over low heat until thickened. Stir small amount into egg yolks. Add to mixture and cook for two minutes. Remove from heat and blend in vanilla, butter, and peanut butter.
3. Fold in the beaten egg whites. Pour mixture into 9" pie shell.

—Alma Bloss, Jackson, Ohio

Hot Milk Sponge Cake

Makes 1 long cake

2 cups sugar
3 eggs, unbeaten
2 cups flour, or 1¾ cups white flour and ¼ cup whole wheat flour
2 tsp. baking powder
1 cup milk, scalding hot

1. In large mixing bowl combine sugar and eggs. Stir with large spoon. Add flour and baking soda. Stir thoroughly. Add scalding hot milk.
2. Bake in long floured cake pan at 350° until cake is done (about 30 minutes). Test with toothpick.
3. Serve warm with strawberries or other fresh or frozen fruit.
Note: Do not use electric mixer. For some reason this cake turns out better done by hand.

My mother used to bake this sponge cake quite often. It is quick to make and can be prepared while you are cooking a meal. We never considered this a "fancy" cake and seldom made it for company, but now I do.

—Sarah Yoder Scott, Newark, Delaware

Golden Angel Food Cake

Makes 18–20 servings

8 egg yolks
1 cup cold water
1½ cups sugar
2 cups whole wheat flour
½ cup cornstarch
½ tsp. salt
1½ tsp. vanilla
8 egg whites
1 tsp. cream of tartar

1. Beat egg yolks until lightly colored. Add cold water and beat for 2 minutes. Add sugar and blend.
2. Combine flour, cornstarch, and salt. Sift 3 or 4 times. Add to egg yolk mixture. Beat 3 or 4 times. Add vanilla.
3. Beat egg whites with cream of tartar until very stiff. Fold into egg yolk mixture. Mix evenly.
4. Bake in angel food cake pan 1¼ hours at 325°. (Fill cake pan to within 1 inch of the top. Bake rest in loaf pan.) Invert pan on pop bottle to cool.

A number of people who do not care for white angel food cake, our son included, have liked this cake since it has more "body" to it.

—Anna Ruth Beck, Halstead, Kansas

Apple Nut Coffee Cake

Makes 1 long cake

½ cup oil
½ cup honey
2 eggs
1 tsp. vanilla
1 cup yogurt or 1 cup sour milk
2 cups whole wheat flour
1 tsp. baking powder

1 tsp. soda
1/4 tsp. salt
2 cups apples, unpeeled and finely chopped

1. Mix oil, honey, eggs, vanilla, and yogurt together well. Add remaining ingredients except apples.
2. Fold in apples.

Topping

1/2 cup chopped nuts
1/4 cup honey
1 tsp. cinnamon
1 Tbsp. oil

1. Drizzle topping onto batter.
2. Bake 30–35 minutes at 350°. Let cool slightly before cutting.

—*Glenda Knepp, Turner, Michigan*

Brownies

Makes 12–16 brownies

2 squares bitter chocolate
1/2 cup butter
1 cup sugar
2 eggs, unbeaten
1 tsp. vanilla
1 cup nuts, broken
3/4 cup flour
1/2 tsp. baking powder
1/2 tsp. salt

1. Melt chocolate and butter together over hot water in double boiler. Add sugar and eggs and beat thoroughly. Continue stirring and add vanilla and nuts.
2. Sift dry ingredients together and stir in thoroughly.
3. Pour into greased 8″ or 9″ square pan. Bake at 350° for 25 minutes. When cool, sprinkle confectioner's sugar on top.

—*Elaine Gibbel, Lititz, Pennsylvania*

Poppy Seed Coffee Cake

Makes 12 servings

> ¹/₂ cup poppy seeds
> 1 cup buttermilk
> ¹/₄ tsp. almond flavoring
> 1 cup butter or margarine
> 1¹/₂ cups sugar
> 4 eggs, separated
> 2¹/₂ cups flour
> 1 tsp. soda
> 1 tsp. baking powder
> pinch salt
> ¹/₂ cup sugar
> 1 Tbsp. cinnamon

1. Combine first three ingredients.
2. Cream butter and 1¹/₂ cups sugar. Add egg yolks.
3. Sift flour, soda, baking powder, and salt together and add alternately with buttermilk mixture to creamed ingredients, beating after each addition.
5. Pour ¹/₄ of batter into each of 2 regular-sized oiled loaf pans.
6. Mix together the ¹/₂ cup sugar and the cinnamon. Sprinkle ¹/₄ of this mixture onto each loaf. Divide rest of batter in half; add to each pan. Sprinkle on the rest of the sugar-cinnamon mixture.
7. Using dinner knife or spatula, cut through the batter in each pan to marbleize.
8. Bake 40–50 minutes at 350°.

Note: This coffee cake can also be baked in a tube pan for 1 hour.

Poppy seed has been a popular and favored ingredient in this community's baking.

—Florence Waltner, Freeman, South Dakota

Rice Pudding, the 5-5-5 Way

5 cups milk
5 Tbsp. rice
5 Tbsp. sugar
dash of salt

1. Mix all ingredients together.
2. Pour into a buttered baking dish.
3. Bake uncovered at 325° for 2 hours, stirring 2 or 3 times.

This is delicious for Sunday evening supper.

—Olive Gross and Geraldine Harder, Lansdale, Pennsylvania

French Flan

Serves 6

1/2 cup sugar
3 large eggs, beaten
1/3 cup sugar
pinch salt
2 cups milk, scalded
1 Tbsp. flour
1/2 tsp. vanilla

1. Heat sugar in heavy skillet. Shake skillet and stir until sugar melts to a golden brown syrup. Immediately pour a little into each of six custard cups, or a 1½-quart baking dish. Working quickly, tilt dishes so caramel coats sides.
2. Combine remaining ingredients in bowl. Beat well. Pour into caramel-coated baking dishes, and set into larger pan of hot water 1 inch deep. Bake 45–50 minutes at 350°. Chill flan. Just before serving, run tip of knife around edges, then unmold into serving dishes. If using larger baking dish, unmold flan onto serving dish, cut in wedges, and spoon a little sauce over each serving.

—Doris Longacre

Apricot Balls

Makes 40 balls

2 8-oz. pkgs. dried apricots
14-oz. pkg. coconut, shredded
1 cup nuts, chopped
1 can sweetened condensed milk
powdered sugar

1. Grind apricots. Add coconut, nuts, and milk. Mix together.
2. Butter hands or use cold water on hands and roll into balls about the size of a walnut. Then roll in powdered sugar.

   These freeze well.

—Betty Linscheid, Hesston, Kansas

Peach Cobbler

4 cups sliced peaches, or any fruit, sweetened or unsweetened,
   fresh, canned or frozen
1 cup whole wheat flour
1 cup unbleached flour
2 tsp. baking powder
2 eggs
½ cup honey
1 tsp. cinnamon
1 cup milk

1. Place peaches in ungreased 9″ x 13″ pan. Stir together the flour and baking powder. Add remaining ingredients and pour over fruit.
2. Bake at 350° for 30 minutes. Serve warm with milk.

—Glenda Knepp, Turner, Michigan

Dried Apple Custard

Makes 6 servings

>2 cups dried apples
>1/2 cup sugar
>1/4 cup brown sugar
>6 egg yolks
>1/2 cup margarine, melted
>1 tsp. vanilla
>1 Tbsp. lemon juice
>6 egg whites
>1/4 tsp. salt

1. Cook apples. Drain. Beat apples, sugars, and salt until smooth. Add egg yolks. Beat in melted margarine. Mixture will be thick. Transfer mixture to double boiler.
2. Stir custard over boiling water for about 6 minutes. Remove from heat. Stir in vanilla and lemon juice. Wash beaters well. In large mixing bowl beat egg whites. Fold in apple mixture. Serve warm or chilled.

Note: Custard will be smoother if apples, sugar, and salt are beaten in blender a few minutes. This will also help break up small particles of peelings if unpeeled dried apples are used.

—Ida Hostetler, Louisville, Ohio

Tropical Bananas

Makes 8 servings

4–6 large, firm, barely ripe bananas
2 Tbsp. fresh lemon or lime juice
1 tsp. lemon or lime peel, grated (optional)
1/2 cup brown sugar
1/8 tsp. ground cloves
1/4 tsp. cinnamon
1/4 tsp. nutmeg
1/4 cup butter or margarine

1. Cut bananas in half lengthwise and crosswise. Place cut-side down in a shallow buttered baking dish.
2. Sprinkle with fruit juice and peel.
3. Mix together sugar and spices and sprinkle over bananas. Then dot with butter.
4. Broil about 5 minutes until golden.
5. Serve as a topping for vanilla ice cream.

—Esther R. Graber, Aibonito, Puerto Rico

Apple Granola

Makes 4 servings

6 cups unpeeled, sliced apples
1 tsp. cinnamon
1 cup rolled oats
1 cup wheat germ
1 cup whole wheat flour
1 cup sunflower seeds
3/4 cup water
1/2 cup honey

1. Place apples in ungreased 9″ x 13″ pan. (A food processor is a fast slicer.) Sprinkle cinnamon over apples.
2. Stir together oats, wheat germ, whole wheat flour and sunflower seeds.

Add water and honey. Spoon over apples.
3. Bake at 350° for 40–45 minutes. Serve warm with milk.

—Glenda Knepp, Turner, Michigan

Ellen's Granola

8 cups rolled oats
1 cup wheat germ
1 cup powdered milk
1 cup shredded coconut
$1/2$ cup soya flour
1 cup sunflower seeds
1 cup chopped nuts
$1/4$ cup sesame seeds
1 cup pumpkin seeds
1 cup oil
1 cup honey
$1/2$ tsp. salt

1. Combine oil and honey and heat thoroughly until blended.
2. Combine dry ingredients. Pour honey/oil mixture over ingredients, mixing thoroughly.
3. Bake at 350° for 30 minutes in a large roasting pan, stirring every 10 minutes. Add raisins or chopped dried fruit as desired. For best results use only old-fashioned, large-flake rolled oats.

—Ellen Helmuth, Debec, New Brunswick

Keith Helmuth's "Regular"

Large soup bowl ¹/₃ filled with Ellen's granola (see page 271)
2 or 3 large dollops of yogurt
Generous topping of applesauce
Add a little honey if you wish it sweeter or a dash of molasses if
you're feeling a bit anemic (iron, you know).

Add milk and gently mix until desired consistency is reached. Omit milk if you prefer the crunchiness of the granola to predominate.

Some years ago in the presence of a lunchtime visitor to our farm, my wife, Ellen, asked if I wanted her to make me a sandwich or if I wanted my "regular." I decided on my "regular" and proceeded to assemble it. Our guest watched the process and at the conclusion said, "I'll have Keith's regular, too." I suspect something like it is a "regular" for a good many folks, but when asked to think of my favorite recipe it is right at the top.

Applesauce is standard for me, but good alternatives are sliced apples, peaches, or pears. Or all three at once if you are in flush times and feeling really decadent. I was even known to use fruit cocktail in my urban days, but the sugar is too much for me now. This is a meal that does equally well for breakfast, lunch, and supper, and I depend on it when Ellen is visiting family in Virginia.

Any granola can be used but, of course, in my opinion there is none better than Ellen's special blend.

—Keith Helmuth, Debec, New Brunswick

Yogurt-Banana Shake

Yogurt

> *2 cups instant dry milk powder*
> *1¹/₂ cups tap water*
> *2 Tbsp. sugar*
> *2 cups boiling water*
> *3–4 Tbsp. plain yogurt*

1. Combine dry milk powder, tap water, and sugar in a bowl. Stir in boiling

water. Add yogurt as a starter. Stir briskly with a wire whisk.
2. Incubate 4–6 hours at 110–120° until set. You can incubate yogurt by placing the covered bowl over a gas stove pilot light in the oven with only the light on, in a covered styrofoam cooler with warm water around the bowl or jar, or in a yogurt maker.
3. Chill at least four hours before serving.

Yogurt Shake

> 1 banana
> 1 cup plain chilled yogurt

Whirl banana and yogurt together in blender about five seconds.

—*Doris Longacre*

Peanutty Popsicles

> 1 Tbsp. carob powder
> 1 Tbsp. unflavored gelatin
> 1 cup boiling water
> 1 cup peanut butter
> 1 cup double strength milk (1 cup milk blended with 1/3 cup
>   instant dry milk)
> 1/3 cup honey
> 1 tsp. vanilla

1. Combine carob powder and unflavored gelatin. Stir to dissolve in boiling water.
2. Add peanut butter, double strength milk, and honey. Stir. Warm over low heat or in microwave until mixed evenly.
3. Add vanilla. Freeze in popsicle molds or paper cups.

—*Glenda Knepp, Turner, Michigan*

Pantry Fudge

2 cups carob chips, sweetened or unsweetened
1 cup peanut butter
2 cups wheat germ, raw or toasted
1 tsp. vanilla (optional)

1. Place carob chips and peanut butter in small bowl. Stir over low heat, or in microwave, until soft.
2. Add wheat germ and vanilla. Mix well. Mixture will be stiff.
3. Place in 9″ square pan. Cut into squares. Refrigerate.

— Glenda Knepp, Turner, Michigan

Cottage Cheese Dip

16 oz. cottage cheese
8 oz. sour cream
1 clove garlic, minced
1 bunch scallions, chopped
celery salt to taste
fresh ground pepper

Combine all ingredients and chill before serving.

— Viola King, Hesston, Kansas

Cape Cod Cooler

Makes 4–6 servings

> **1 tea bag**
> **3 cups water, boiling**
> **¹/₃ cup sugar**
> **1 cup cranberry juice cocktail**
> **1 Tbsp. lemon juice**

1. Brew tea in hot water 3–5 minutes.
2. Remove tea bag and add sugar, stirring until dissolved.
3. Pour into pitcher. Stir in cranberry and lemon juices. Serve over ice.

> *—A family recipe from Miriam Meyer, Olive Gross, and*
> *Geraldine Harder, Lansdale, Pennsylvania*

Orange Tea Cooler

> **¹/₂ cup instant tea powder**
> **12-oz. can frozen orange juice concentrate**
> **¹/₂ cup honey**

Combine ingredients in gallon container. Fill partially with water, stirring to blend. Finish filling with water and ice. Stir. Serve cool over ice.

> *—Glenda Knepp, Turner, Michigan*

Index

About the Author

Phyllis Pellman Good, a Lancaster County, Pennsylvania, native, first discovered that she was a Pennsylvania Dutch cook when she drew a curious audience in a dorm kitchen in New York City one evening while preparing Chicken Corn Soup. She has since authored **Cooking and Memories** and co-authored **From Amish and Mennonite Kitchens.**

Today Phyllis spends much of her time as a book editor. She also edits **Festival Quarterly,** a magazine exploring the art, faith, and culture of Mennonite peoples. She is co-editor of the book **Perils of Professionalism** and co-editor with her husband, Merle, of **20 Most Asked Questions about the Amish and Mennonites.**

Together she and Merle are executive directors of The People's Place, The Old Country Store, and several associated shops in Intercourse, Pennsylvania.

Phyllis received her B.A. and M.A. in English from New York University.

The Goods are the parents of two daughters and members of the Landisville Mennonite Church, Landisville, Pennsylvania.

Notes

Notes